Rich Christia

Rich Christians, Poor Christians

Monica Hill

Marshall Pickering

Marshall Morgan and Scott
Marshall Pickering
34–42 Cleveland Street, London, W1P 5FB. U.K.

First published in 1989 by Marshall Morgan and Scott
Publications Ltd.

Part of the Marshall Pickering Holdings Group

British Library Cataloguing in Publication Data
Hill, Monica, *1934–*
   Rich Christians, poor Christians.
   1. Christian life. Spirituality
   I. Title
248.4

ISBN: 0 551 01898-4

Text Set in Baskerville by Prima Graphics, Camberley, Surrey
Printed in Great Britain by Collins, Glasgow

Contents

Foreword   vii

1 WHO ARE THE RICH?   1

2 PERSECUTION   10

3 SHAKING AND REVIVAL   35

4 GROWTH IN NUMBERS   60

5 SPIRITUAL POWER   90

6 PROPHETIC WITNESS   115

7 COMMUNITY CONSCIOUSNESS   139

8 WHAT ABOUT THE POOR?   165

Rich Christians, Poor Christians

Monica Hill

A tape containing additional material and guidance for group discussion has been prepared to supplement this book. It is available from the British Church Growth Association, St Marks Chambers, Kennington Park Road, LONDON SE11 4PW; price £3.00 including postage.

Foreword

This book brings together first-hand stories of the work and witness of Christians in many different lands. It gives up-to-date and factual information of the growth of the church worldwide, and thrilling examples of the power of God at work in some of the poorest countries.

The great value of this book is that Monica writes out of her own experience of travel and ministry in many different parts of the world which she combines with her work as Executive Officer of the British Church Growth Association. This has given her some unique insights into the way God is working out his purposes in this generation and how the Gospel continues to turn the values of the world upside-down.

Why is it that the power of God is to be seen at work so mightily among some of the world's poorest people? What's gone wrong in the West with its rich heritage of biblical tradition? Who are the poor?

You will not be the same after you've read this book. It is compelling reading that will inspire, challenge and widen your vision. But above all it will open your eyes to what God is doing in his world today.

Dr Clifford Hill

Chapter One

Who are the Rich?

Has not God chosen those who are poor in the eyes of the world to be rich in faith, and to inherit the kingdom he promised those who love him?

James 2:5

The Faith Spreads

The Western nations have, for many years, considered themselves to be the major missionaries of Christ, commissioned to take the Gospel throughout the world as well as being the custodians of the true faith for which they have felt an urgency, even a divine right, to pass on to others. They have understood their destiny to be to *give* the Gospel to others rather than to *receive* anything from anyone else.

During the nineteenth and twentieth centuries Christians from all over Europe and North America responded enthusiastically to the Great Commission and helped take the seed of the Gospel around the world accompanied by, and accompanying, colonisation and the establishing of Empires under the control of the rich industrial nations of the West. At the beginning of the twentieth century, Christians in the Western nations greatly outnumbered those in the non-West. Today the position has been reversed and the number of Christians in non-western nations is now greater than those in the nations of the West. Western missionaries, nevertheless, are still the most numerous, particularly those from the United States of America. It is also interesting to note that pentecostal and charismatic missionaries have now risen to 28 per cent of the total of those serving the church overseas.

The churches in the developing nations are taking mission seriously, although many of them do not have the physical resources of the western Church. It will not be long before the western nations - affluent though they may still be in material things but where all too often the Christian presence is declining - are the recipients of a mission strategy programme initiated from the other side of the world.

David Barratt, in the *World Christian Encyclopedia*, tells us that whereas at the beginning of the twentieth century 65 per cent of all Christians in the world were from the richer western nations and only 17 per cent from the poorer 'two-thirds world', by 1988 this proportion had practically reversed; the former having dropped to 39 per cent and the latter risen to 53 per cent. An even greater swing has been projected for the end of this century when the comparative figures are expected to be 32 per cent and 61 per cent. God is doing a new thing in countries not having the material possessions that western Christians have taken for granted for so many years. The poor are being mightily blessed with spiritual riches while the rich are being sent empty away, which is what Mary foresaw in her song of praise (Luke 1:53).

Rich or Poor

On what basis should Christians judge who is rich and who is poor? It is not difficult to answer that question in secular terms, since wealth and power are inseparably linked among the nations of the world. The industrialised nations of the West have a monopoly of wealth and power, whereas the developing nations are struggling with poverty and debt. But when it comes to spiritual matters, who are the rich?

The Bible gives a clear answer to this question. In the Old Testament material prosperity is seen as a sign of God's blessing since all things come from him. Nevertheless God does not favour the rich – 'Rich and poor have this in common: The Lord is the Maker of them all' (Proverbs 22:2), and Elihu observes to Job in 34:19 that God 'shows no partiality to princes and does not favour the rich over the poor, for they are all the work of his hands.'

Material riches are not a criterion of God's favour, and should not be the reason why men or women are honoured. 'Do not be overawed when a man grows rich, when the splendour of his house increases; for he will take nothing with him when he dies' (Psalm 49:16–17). Riches do not last, they have no permanent value and neither does 'a man who has riches without understanding. He is like the beasts that perish' (v20).

Material Riches
In fact riches can be a hindrance to spiritual growth and they bring many problems which are not experienced by those who have no riches. 'The sleep of a labourer is sweet, whether he eats little or much, but the abundance of a rich man permits him no sleep' (Eccl. 5:12); 'Whoever loves money never has money enough; whoever loves wealth is never satisfied with his income' (Eccl. 5:10), and Proverbs 11:28 warns, 'Whoever trusts in his riches will fall.'

Prosperity was often the cause of apostasy in the history of Israel. The Lord's indignation against the fickleness of his people when riches came is conveyed by Hosea – 'I am the Lord your God who brought you out of Egypt . . . I cared for you in the desert . . . When I fed them, they were satisfied; when they were satisfied, they became proud; then they forgot me' (13:4–6). This statement summarises in a single sentence the spiritual history of Israel, and underlines the dangers of prosperity. When they were in need, God fed them. They soon grew satisfied and took God's blessings for granted. They became self-satisfied and

3

proud. Then they turned their backs upon God and began to worship the false gods of the other nations.

It was no doubt with this in mind that Agur pleaded with God, 'give me neither poverty nor riches, but give me only my daily bread. Otherwise, I may have too much and disown you and say, "Who is the Lord?" Or I may become poor and steal, and so dishonour the name of my God' (Proverbs 30:8-9).

The teaching of the Bible is not that riches in themselves are wrong, but that the pursuit of riches is harmful, and the love of riches is evil. Solomon was commended for not asking God for wealth or any other worldly values, but even though he did not ask, these things were given to him as an extra gift from God (2 Chron. 1:11-12). 'Humility and the fear of the Lord bring wealth and honour and life' (Proverbs 22:4).

The major charge that the prophets of Israel brought against the rich was that they misused their material prosperity. Instead of using their power and their wealth for the benefit of the community they became oppressors of the poor. Amos cried out against the rich, 'Hear this, you who trample the needy and do away with the poor of the land... buying the poor with silver and the needy for a pair of sandals... I will turn your religious feasts into mourning and all your singing into weeping' (Amos 8:4-10). Similarly, Micah declared, 'He has showed you, O man, what is good. And what does the Lord require of you? To act justly and to love mercy and to walk humbly with your God' (Micah 6:8).

Isaiah speaks scathingly of the way in which the rich were using their wealth to drive the poor from the land. 'Woe to you who add house to house and join field to field till no space is left and you live alone in the land' (Isaiah 5:8). God hates those who exploit their workers and oppress the powerless. The kind of behaviour he is looking for is 'to share your food with the hungry and to provide the poor wanderer with

4

shelter – when you see the naked, to clothe him.' He says that 'if you spend yourselves on behalf of the hungry and satisfy the needs of the oppressed, then your light will rise in the darkness... the Lord will guide you always; he will satisfy your needs' (Isaiah 58:3-12).

Spiritual Priorities

Jesus came to earth not only to accomplish our salvation, but also to turn upside down the values of this world. His teaching on many issues, especially on wealth and poverty, must have seemed revolutionary to those who heard him. In the Sermon on the Mount, he said, 'blessed are the poor for theirs is the kingdom of God, and woe to those who are rich for they have already received their comfort' (Luke 6:20-26). This was a foretaste of teaching which was designed to encourage spiritual rather than material values.

Jesus told a parable of the rich man who built bigger and bigger barns and took great pride in his possessions, but who died in spiritual poverty leaving all his wealth behind (Luke 12:16-21). Jesus showed the stupidity of putting trust in worldly things. God is more concerned with how we use our possessions, large or small. So Jesus commended the poor widow who put all she had into the temple offering box because of her love for God (Mark 12:41-44). He is the one who gives to us, and we are stewards of his resources. We therefore have a duty to use them rightly and we will be accountable to God for our actions.

Jesus told a powerful parable about a poor rich man named Dives who died and went to hell, and a rich poor man named Lazarus who died and went to heaven. He said that Dives had received his good things during his lifetime whereas Lazarus had been a beggar at the rich man's gate 'longing to eat what fell from the rich man's table' (Luke 16:21). Now the positions were reversed. In the teaching of Jesus, the

5

injustices of this life are to be corrected in the life-hereafter. His advice was 'do not store up for yourselves treasures on earth, where moth and rust destroy, and where thieves break in and steal. But store up for yourselves treasure in heaven . . . where your treasure is, there your heart will be also' (Matt. 6:19–21).

The Bible sees earthly riches as a responsibility and even a hazard; their very presence can encourage us to forget God. We can become greedy wanting more and more – never satisfied. Wealth becomes addictive like a drug – we crave for more, it dominates the whole of life and blinds us to spiritual things and even to the value of love and family. The pursuit of wealth eats like a cancer into the soul of man, and the end is spiritual death just as surely as physical cancer, unless treated, leads to physical death.

When the rich young man came to Jesus for advice on how to attain eternal life, the one thing he could not do was give up his wealth. Jesus used this to teach his disciples about the great difficulty facing those with wealth who want to enter the Kingdom of heaven, even if they were morally and religiously righteous. Matthew records that the disciples were amazed at this teaching – if someone like this upright young man could not be admitted, how could anyone be saved! (Matt. 19:16–25).

What then are the riches for which we should strive? Paul in his first letter to Timothy told him to, 'command those who are rich in this present world not to be arrogant nor to put their hope in wealth, which is so uncertain, but to put their hope in God, who richly provides us with everything for our enjoyment. Command them to do good, to be rich in good deeds and to be generous and willing to share. In this way they will lay up treasure for themselves as a firm foundation for the coming age, so that they may take hold of the life that is truly life' (6:17–19).

James goes even further and warns the rich and the

oppressors, 'Now listen, you rich people, weep and wail because of the misery that is coming upon you. Your wealth has rotted, and moths have eaten your clothes . . . you have hoarded wealth in the last days. Look! The wages you failed to pay the workmen who mowed your fields are crying out against you' (James 5:1-4).

He reverses the natural order of self-pride telling the 'brother in humble circumstances to take pride in his high position. But the one who is rich should take pride in his low position' (James 1:9-10).

Spiritual Values
Paul tried to communicate God's spiritual riches as the 'incomparable riches of his grace expressed in his kindness to us in Christ Jesus' (Eph. 2:7); he spoke about the riches of the wisdom and knowledge of God which were continually being revealed to man (Romans 11:33); and of the riches of complete understanding in order that those (particularly in Colossi and Laodicea) 'may know the mystery of God, namely Christ, in whom are hidden all the treasures of wisdom and knowledge' (Col. 2:2).

It is ironic that only a few years later John was writing to those same Laodiceans (Rev. 3:14-22) one of the most devastating messages to any of the churches in Asia Minor. They were apathetic, 'neither hot nor cold', and they did not realise how much they were anathema to God – so much so that he was about to spit them out of his mouth. 'You say, "I am rich; I have acquired wealth and do not need a thing." But you do not realise that you are wretched, pitiful, poor, blind and naked.' He told them that God rebukes and disciplines those whom he loves, and wants them to repent of their waywardness and to reverse their spiritual state of poverty, blindness and nakedness. They could, and should, do this by 'buying gold refined in the fire, so that you can become rich; and white clothes to wear, so you can cover your shameful

7

nakedness; and salve to put on your eyes, so you can see'.

We do not know whether the warning was heeded in time to strengthen the church before the persecution of the Roman Empire broke upon them, but we do know that there is no church in Laodicea now. In fact none of the seven churches of Asia Minor to whom John addressed his urgent warnings from the Holy Spirit have survived.

The message of the Spirit to the church at Laodicea is one that the rich nations of the West urgently need to hear and to heed. Any nation which sees itself as rich and no longer needing anything from God is in great danger. That nation needs to apply the same eye ointment that John recommended to the Laodiceans so that they could clearly see their true spiritual condition.

Conversely, the message sent to the church in Smyrna (Rev. 2:8-11), which was suffering persecution and poverty, was one of great encouragement. The believers were not to be afraid of the problems facing them, because God was with them. Although they were poor in worldly wealth and power, in God's eyes they were rich, and the power of the Spirit of God was available to them. If they were faithful they would receive the crown of life.

It is not difficult to recognise the relevance of these messages for our world today. There are many churches in the West which were once spiritually rich and enjoyed the blessing of God but who, although still materially rich, are now spiritually poor. They need to heed the warnings of God although their ears are not open to hear. In contrast, there are many Christians in the materially poor nations of the world who have great spiritual riches, and from whom the western church can learn.

When we look at the churches in the light of Biblical teaching, the questions 'Who are the rich?' and 'Who are the poor?' have a very different answer than if we judge by the standards of the world. The rich are the poor and the poor are the rich. The values of the Kingdom turn upside down the values of the world.

Questions

1 How much do we allow the world to influence our values? Do we live by worldly standards comparing ourselves with others living around us, or do we look for other standards on which to base our lives? In what do we put our trust? What material possessions do we value highly – how would we cope if all material possessions were removed?

2 We read how, in biblical times (Hosea 13:6 and Proverbs 30:8-9), it was recognised that material riches led to a turning away from God. Do you think this still happens today? Do material riches always seem to lead to apathy and a turning away from spiritual things? Can it be avoided? How?

3 Read again James 1:9-10. What does this mean? How should the poor take pride in their high position and the rich take pride in their lowly position?

4 Jesus often taught in a revolutionary way by reversing the values of the world to put forward spiritual values. We have been noting in this chapter how he called the rich 'poor' and the poor 'rich'. Can you discover other examples of the way in which Jesus' teaching turned upside down the values of the world?

Chapter Two

Persecution

Blessed are those who are persecuted because of righteousness, for theirs is the kingdom of heaven.
Matthew 5:10

Rich Christians

Persecution of Christians is not new – it is as old as the church. It began soon after Pentecost with the clampdown of the authorities in Jerusalem following the murder of Stephen. There probably has never been a period in history when the church has not experienced persecution because the very nature of the Gospel brings the church into conflict with the world.

Today there is evidence that the number of Christian martyrs throughout the world is increasing. David Barratt in the *World Christian Encyclopedia* estimates that approximately 330,000 Christians are martyred worldwide each year. This is a staggering total. Persecutions may not be evident in western nations where religious tolerance is part of state policy and is extended to people of all faiths, including cults and secularists, but in many non-western nations persecution exists either openly or more covertly in the form of restrictive regulations or where the authorities turn a blind eye to mob violence.

Chinese Policy
In China, the persecution of Christians is part of official state policy towards those in unregistered

churches. On 31 March 1982, the Party Central Committee, the highest governing body in China, issued *Document 19* entitled *Concerning Our Country's Position and Policy On Religious Questions During the Socialist Period.* The document recognises three designates. They are:

1 designated pastoral personnel,
2 designated places of worship, and
3 designated parishes.

Preachers have to be officially licenced by the state, worship can only take place in church buildings approved by the government for religious activities, and designated parishes are those districts in which registered personnel may carry out their religious duties. *Document 19* calls for severe punishment of non-designated personnel – it names them as 'counter-revolutionaries and criminals who act under the cover of religion'. Section 11 of *Document 19* states that a close watch should be kept on house churches and that they should be regarded as underground movements hostile to the objectives of socialism in China. The Chinese authorities regard the purpose of the underground churches as being 'espionage and sabotage under the cover of religion'.

Despite these strict regulations and the punishment of offenders, the House Church Movement continues to flourish throughout China. Untold numbers of pastors refuse to register with the authorities, and continue to hold illegal services in houses because they refuse to accept the restrictions imposed upon the officially recognised churches. These include a prohibition on all forms of evangelism, including sharing belief within the family, and, among the restrictions on preaching, reference to the Second Coming of Christ is prohibited.

There are untold numbers of house church leaders, pastors and evangelists in the rapidly growing underground church in China, who have suffered persecution

11

at the hands of the authorities attempting to stop the spread of Christianity. But still the faith spreads, and the authorities are left frustrated and embarrassed because of the fearless witness of outstanding Christian leaders. Two such men are evangelist Xu Yongze and pastor Lin Xiangao (Samuel Lam).

Xu Yongze

Xu Yongze is an itinerant evangelist who planted more than 3,000 churches between 1980 and 1988 while travelling throughout central and northern China. He went from village to village preaching the Gospel, and establishing churches. Since 1983 he has been pursued by the Chinese authorities for allegedly illegally propagating the Christian faith, and for leading an 'unregistered' Christian organisation. In 1988 he went to Beijing where he was to meet Dr Billy Graham, but the day before that meeting his presence in the city became known and he was arrested. The authorities refused to give any information concerning his arrest, and would not even confirm that he was held in captivity. He simply disappeared from sight.

Lin Ziangao

Lin Ziangao (Samuel Lam) is pastor of a house church in Guangzhou, the capital city of Canton province. He was imprisoned for a total of more than twenty-one years. Prior to the 1949 Communist revolution, he had been pastor of a church which was closed at that time. But he continued preaching to a congregation of about 300 until his arrest in 1955 when he was imprisoned for one year and four months. On his release he began preaching again and was re-arrested two years later. He was charged with being an anti-revolutionary, and was sentenced to twenty years in a labour camp. Chinese labour camps are not easy places. Many of them are large, often a day's walk from one side to the other, and the work is hard and dangerous. Samuel was sent to a coal mine to serve his time.

During his first imprisonment, Samuel Lam's Bible had been taken away from him, and this experience taught him the value of memory. He had used the time he was free to memorise many of the Psalms and his favourite passages from the prophets and the Gospels – such as Isaiah 53 and John 14–17. When he was re-arrested he maintained his faith by quietly reciting the memorised passages. He recalls how close he felt to God, and knew that he was being preserved for a purpose. There were many incidents when his life was in danger, which confirmed his conviction that God was in control. On one such occasion, a runaway truck came straight for him when he was backed up against the rocks, but it jammed against the wall beside him and he was unscathed.

During this time he met a fellow prisoner who was also a pastor and who still had a New Testament in his possession. He shared this with Samuel, and each time it came into the latter's hands he memorised another passage preparing himself for the day when he knew he would be totally deprived again of the precious word. In this way, he memorised all the Epistles from Romans to Hebrews. Eventually, the guards discovered the Bible and burnt it. For punishment, the two Christians were separated and Samuel was sent to another prison. But God works in all things for good, and here Samuel obtained pencil and paper, and laboriously wrote out – from memory and in Chinese characters – the whole of Paul's Epistles.

He was also given a new job – that of prison camp barber! The Communist guards did not realise how they were furthering the Gospel by giving him access to each man in the camp. One by one they came and sat in his chair to have their hair cut and receive his individual attention! Samuel eagerly seized this ideal opportunity for evangelism. As he cut their hair, he whispered the Gospel into their ears; many became believers.

In 1976, two years before his release, Samuel's wife died so he never saw her again. In his own words, he had nothing else to live for but Christ. To his great surprise, when he came out of prison in 1978, he was allowed to return to his home in the back streets of his native Guangzhou.

Obviously he could not re-open his church and so had to find other means of earning a living. But the doors into China were beginning to open to the West, and people wanted to learn English. Having learnt to speak English before the revolution when he studied at the Alliance Bible College in inland China, Samuel opened his home for English lessons. In 1979, he enrolled his first four students, all girls, and after each lesson he would share his faith with them. All four became believers, and he baptised them in 1980 in the local river. The following week, one of the students took her cousin to Samuel's house, and so his congregation became five. Between 1980 and 1986, he baptised 900 new believers!

In 1987 when I visited Samuel Lam, his house church had a congregation of about 600. They were still meeting in his tiny home, and, on the weekday evening that I visited him, the house was full of people – on all three floors. They were sitting wherever they could find room, even on the stairs, all eager to learn more about the faith. Each night of the week there are Bible studies, training classes or prayer meetings. His home is totally given over to the Lord . I noticed a tiny bed roll under some chairs in a back room; it appeared to be his only personal possession.

Of course his home could not possibly accommodate 600 people all at one time, but 200 do manage to pack in three times each Sunday. That, alone, is hard enough to imagine. This number is twenty times above the legal limit; it is illegal to hold a meeting of

14

more than ten persons without the permission of the authorities. Samuel's house church has been ransacked by the police on many occasions, and he has lost precious Bibles and song books, but still he persists in his ministry.

Samuel's church has continued to grow, and by 1988 he had baptised more than 1,000, and had a regular congregation of 800 still meeting in his home. One third of all those he has baptised have gone out as travelling evangelists and pastors all over China. But the authorities could no longer turn a blind eye to his activities, and towards the end of 1988 he was arrested again for holding an illegal meeting. He was warned that he must register his church or suffer closure. At the time of writing, he was still defying the authorities and continuing to evangelise and to pastor his church.

Asked if he were not afraid of the authorities, Samuel responded, 'They have done everything they can to me except take my life – and I am ready for that.'

Persecution has had the effect of strengthening the faith of Christians in China. There are many men and women, today, willing to die for the Gospel. I was concerned for Samuel Lam's personal safety even in reporting his story, but he welcomed the opportunity to share news of what is happening. In 1988, Billy Graham visited the church and took with him a message of encouragement from the President of the United States. There is no doubt that if Pastor Lam were executed or imprisoned it would cause an outcry in the West. But he himself is prepared to make the ultimate sacrifice for his Lord if called to do so, and in the meantime he believes that by bringing the whole situation into the open and challenging the authorities, he can best further the Gospel in China.

Romanian Faith
It seems a strange anomaly that persecution can actually strengthen personal faith and further the

Gospel in a nation. Yet this has been the experience of Christians throughout the centuries. It is not only in China, but in many other parts of the world that persecution of Christians is taking place. In Eastern Europe, Joseph Ton made a witness for his faith in his home country of Romania during the time he was minister of the Second Baptist Church in Oradea. He had returned to Romania in 1972 after completing his education at Oxford, and witnessed fearlessly until he was exiled by the government in 1981.

It is not easy being a Christian in Romania: as well as physical hardship caused by the denial of adequate food rations, medical care, fuel and accommodation, people often have to accept demotion in their jobs when they profess Christ. Joseph tells how a man in an important position came to him to be baptised knowing that the authorities would 'almost immediately hold a public meeting to expose him as a backward creature and have him publicly demoted'. He sought advice on how to defend himself during the five minutes they would give him to state his case. Joseph's advice was, 'Brother, defending yourself is the one thing you should *not* do. This is your unique chance to tell them who you were before, and what Jesus made of you; who Jesus is and what he is to you now.' This advice did not prevent him from being denounced nor from losing his position of authority in the factory, but it did open the eyes of his workmates. A little while later he went to Joseph rejoicing in the fact that wherever he walked in the factory someone would come up to him and whisper, 'Give me the address of your church', or 'Tell me more about Jesus', or 'Do you have a Bible for me?'

Joseph Ton's own understanding of martyrdom and persecution came as he studied the New Testament church's approach. He moved from being a low-key Christian concerned for survival and accepting all the restrictions the authorities might put on him because

16

he wanted to live, to one who realised the enormous power he held by being ready to die. He preached uninhibitedly and wrote paper after paper, making tape after tape, and of course harassment and arrests followed. In his own words, 'One day during an interrogation an officer threatened to kill me. Then I said, "Sir, let me explain that issue to you. Your supreme weapon is killing. My supreme weapon is dying. Sir, you know my sermons are all over the country on tapes now. If you kill me, I will be sprinkling them with my blood. Whoever listens to them after that will say, "I'd better listen. This man sealed it with his blood.' So, go and kill me. I win the supreme victory then." He sent me home.'

For years Joseph has wanted to save his life, and was losing it; now he wanted to lose his life, he was winning it. He had learnt about freedom in Christ to do whatever Christ wanted him to do in Romania.

Poor Christians

Modern examples of the persecution of Christians could be repeated from all over the world. The one exception would be the western nations where Christianity has been the traditional religion for centuries. The Christian faith is endemic to the life of all the western nations, and the church holds a unique position in society which has been virtually unchallenged for centuries. The last thing which Christians in the western world expect is persecution.

In Britain, Christianity became so much a part of our culture that it was almost synonymous with being British. Our monarchs are head of the state church, and take their coronation oaths on the Bible. Christianity is, or has been, the official religion with all the privileges that that brings. Church and state are closely linked as part of our heritage. Our system of law and government is based upon biblical principles.

Our social institutions such as 'family' and 'education' have been moulded by Christian patterns and standards. In such a favourable climate the church prospered, and it seemed inconceivable to many that Christians could be persecuted in Britain or in any of the other major western nations.

But the old adage, 'church prosperous, church polluted; church persecuted, church pure' is not easily reversed, and often pollution creeps up unawares on a complacent, unchallenged church. People become Christians because it seems the natural thing to do rather than because they have a real change of heart and consciously embrace the Christian faith. The message and the challenge of the Gospel become blunted to accommodate the desire for security and well-being. Life can be lived without the need for a strong personal faith. Thus the urge to evangelise disappears, and the Gospel becomes incorporated into a largely secular culture.

In Britain today we regard martyrs as belonging to the past when times were not so favourable for Christians. Not only do we have no expectation of persecution, but neither does the ordinary Christian have any expectation of spiritual revival sweeping the nation or of the deep commitment and vibrant faith which usually accompany the experience of persecution. Often we fall back on a kind of 'remnant' ideology, and try to measure our success and growth in other terms while our numbers are in decline. Many are turning away from the traditional religion that we have tried to preserve, but which has become increasingly irrelevant in a secular age. It is inevitable that Christianity will appear irrelevant to secular materialists who have not caught the vision of the Gospel.

Another factor to be taken into consideration for understanding the present situation in Britain is that we are a multi-faith society. Until Sikh, Muslim and Hindu immigrants from India and Pakistan began arriving in Britain in the 1960s, there were very few who wished to opt out of the traditional belief system, which was sanctioned by law and hallowed by custom. The 1944 Education Act laid down the requirement for every child to receive in schools, religious instruction in the Christian faith unless specifically withdrawn. The social pressures of conformity were so strong that many Jewish children and those from humanist families attended, without question, Christian lessons based on the teaching of Scripture.

During the war there was no place for the atheist; everyone in the British Army was either Christian or Jew. If a man said he was agnostic he was recorded as Church of England! Even now, in our post-Christian secular environment, there is plenty of evidence of Christian practices and belief in all our institutions, such as Parliament, which begins each day with prayers. Most people still marry in church, and everyone has to have a religious burial.

In Britain, freedom is valued above all things. It is enshrined in our traditional songs – 'Britain never, never, never shall be slaves'. Even when the slave trade was at its height in the colonies, it was never acceptable on British soil. Any slaves brought here were automatically and immediately manumitted. The basic concept of freedom was instituted by law in the concept of *habeus corpus* and the rights of each individual. In terms of religion, the freedom to believe also carries with it the freedom not to believe and the freedom to believe in other religions. In Britain, we find it difficult to conceive it being otherwise – belief would not be belief if there were no choice.

Alongside the belief in freedom has grown the value of tolerance and the rejection of any form of persecution of minority groups. The British distrust fanaticism which moulds attitudes towards extremist views. For example, most English Christians regard Dr Ian Paisley's staunch Protestantism as bigotry, and, similarly, even British evangelicals would be wary of being identified with American fundamentalism and the Moral Majority Movement.

Western Persecution of the Future
Despite the long-established tradition of tolerance in Britain, there are, however, increasing signs of mounting opposition to the Gospel in Britain today. This may develop into the persecution of the church in the not too distant future. Such a statement would have been inconceivable a generation ago, but the social revolution that has taken place in Britain since the 1950s, together with the onslaught of secularism, is producing an increasingly hostile climate for Christianity.

In the religious and morally permissive society which has grown up in the second half of this century there has also developed a brand of militant secularism which is fighting for the rights of minority groups. The three most powerful movements are those seeking equal rights for women, racial equality and equality for homosexuals. The first two of these were causes traditionally supported by Christians. It was devout Christians, such as William Wilberforce and his friends, who campaigned throughout the late eighteenth and early nineteenth centuries for the abolition of slavery and the emancipation of slaves throughout the British Empire. Even in the second half of the twentieth century when race relations became a social issue at home gaining the attention of politicians, the National Committee for Commonwealth Immigrants, predecessor of the current Commission for Racial Equality, was headed by the Archbishop of Canterbury, and included a number of Christian leaders. It was also Christians who were prominent in the earlier part of this century in campaigning for the franchise for women that led to the vote being extended to them in 1922. Both these movements today have become largely politicised and have moved away from any recognition of Christian roots.

But the real significance of the change of leadership and direction of these movements, lies in the fact that the movements are now seen by many as the new champions of freedom. This was a role traditionally undertaken by Christians and based upon Gospel principles of equality. The new secular champions of freedom not only lack biblical principles but are prepared to adopt almost any means to achieve their ends – even if this means the denial of the rights of others. It is this attitude of militant opposition towards those who are regarded as the upholders of traditional morality that may well develop into the persecution of Christians.

A good example of this is to be seen in the rapid growth during the last two decades of the 'Gay Rights Movement'. This movement set out to change social attitudes towards homosexuals whose activities were legalised in 1968 but who were still regarded as the pariahs of society. Their aim has been to present the image of homosexuals as one of happy gay people who deserve the support of the community in their fight for freedom from biblical concepts of the family and morality. They want to alter the structure of society to include the recognition of homosexual relationships as being equal to the traditional hetero-sexual family. They have been joined by some homo-sexual clergy who also want to see Christian concepts of family and morality changed.

In order to obtain what they consider to be their rights they are demanding positive discrimination in their favour. Some local authorities have introduced equal opportunity policies which favour homosexuals and discriminate against those who stand for traditional morality. A number of churches and Christian organi-sations in Britain have lost their support from public funds because of their refusal to employ practising homosexuals in playgroups, youth work and other social activities or for their refusal to teach about homosexual lifestyles to children under five years old. The fear that the persecution of Christians in Britain may soon become a reality could, therefore, be well founded.

The Gay Rights Movement is also strong in other European nations, particularly in the Netherlands and Scandinavia. In Norway, the homosexual lobby has been strong enough to ensure the passing of a law that not only protects them from discrimination but also makes it illegal to speak against homosexual practices. As secular humanists increasingly gain power in Britain and in other European nations they will undoubtedly use it for the persecution of those who take their stand against moral permissiveness and are therefore regarded as the enemies of freedom.

Historical Perspectives

Religious Persecution

Persecution has been the experience of the church throughout history. It is, however, only in the twentieth century that persecution of Christians has come from secular sources. In previous centuries, persecution was religious, first by the Jews followed by the Roman persecution under Diocletian (also religious because the Christians would not worship the Roman gods). Persecution was always either from non-Christian religious sources, such as Islam, or the persecution of Christians by other Christians.

There are many instances of the ruling group imposing their religious beliefs on others, and persecuting those who refused to conform. But the most severe persecutions have come from within the church by fanatical adherents of different Christian churches with different doctrinal beliefs.

Queen Mary burnt Protestants and enforced Papacy;

a policy that was reversed by her half-sister, Elizabeth I, who persecuted Catholics. Cromwell also burnt Catholics and enforced a stern Puritanism on the people, including the people of Catholic Ireland.

Every new expression of Christianity has been persecuted by those who did not want to accept the new teaching or new emphasis on biblical truth. It is only with the passage of time that tolerance has grown.

In the seventeenth century, the Pilgrim Fathers, who became the founding fathers of the USA, left British shores to build a new life for themselves based upon the word of God. They had been persecuted for their faith in Britain, finding if difficult to continue to live and worship in the intolerant atmosphere of that day which recognised only one brand of Christianity – that of the Church of England.

In the eighteenth century, non-conformists were regarded as those who refused to accept the authority of the state church. John Wesley was persecuted by the Church for deviating from standard practice and although he remained an Anglican all his life, his followers broke away to form Methodism, ostracised by the church.

In the nineteenth century, the Salvation Army were seen as deviationists, and ordinary people were stirred up by righteous Anglicans, with the sanction of the church, to throw stones at them. This ceased only when the poor realised that the Salvation Army was on their side and would do more for them than the traditional church!

In the twentieth century, the Pentecostals were called heretics for their emphasis on spiritual gifts and the power of the Holy Spirit. They were really only accepted by other Christians as the Charismatic movement gained recognition in the 1970s, half a century after the formation of the first Pentecostal churches.

The Reformation was a time of persecution in central and northern Europe. The followers of both Luther and Calvin suffered a great deal. In Britain, the Independents and Puritans were persecuted. Hardly a nation in Europe was spared the traumas of internal conflict. Yet it was also a time of great growth for the church. It seems that the Gospel thrives in a conflict situation; when there is no conflict, decline sets in. It usually begins with complacency, followed by apathy, followed by decline.

The Church has traditionally seen herself as the custodian of truth, and any variations from established doctrine have usually been rejected. This still happens today although rather more gently. New movements are usually despised, denounced as cults or marginalised to such an extent that they are considered to be of no importance. But in Britain it is the newer churches that are gaining ground while, at the same time, the traditional churches are losing social significance. Their power to persecute the new churches no longer exists even if they should wish to do so.

Social Persecution
The new persecution from secular sources that is beginning to be experienced by the Church today had its roots in the nineteenth century. It began with the opposition to the Church and Christianity which came from the intelligentsia – the scientific Darwinians and the social Darwinians. They used argument – polite argument – and their opposition was conceptual rather than of a violent nature and it gained ground in moulding the thinking and 'mindset' of the people. This paved the way for the secular persecution noted above.

There are lessons that can be learnt from history where the Church has enjoyed the favour of, and become too closely associated with the government of a nation. When the winds of change blow, this close association can spell the death knell of the Church or at best rejection and persecution. This happened in

24

Ethiopia where a Christian government was replaced by communists, and in the Sudan where Christians were replaced by Muslims. In both these countries, the change of government has resulted in the persecution of Christians and loss of status for the Church.

A number of African nations, upon obtaining their independence from European overlords, have rejected Christianity because of its links with western imperialism.

The Church in Indonesia is currently enjoying a period of growth despite opposition from the State. The government is Islamic, and although there is officially freedom of religion there are many restrictions placed upon Christian evangelism, and many subtle ways in which the work of the church is hindered. There is, however, very little open persecution of Christians. As long as Christian fanaticism is restrained and the laws of the land are observed, the government is prepared to tolerate the Church. In Indonesia the Muslims have realised that whenever they persecute the Christians the Church grows stronger!

Persecution in the Early Church
The history of the early Church shows that persecution and martyrdom were the seeds of the growth. In fact, the great theologian, Tertullian who was converted when he saw Christians singing as they went out to die, said, 'The blood of the martyrs is the seed of the church'. Augustine tells us that, 'The martyrs were bound, jailed, scourged, wracked, burned, rent, butchered – and still they multiplied.' Throughout the history of the Church, martyrs have always been highly honoured. In the early Church, martyrdom was sometimes sought after by some Christians. In fact some had to be rebuked by the Church and told that if a person provoked his own martyrdom it did not provide him with a place in heaven.

Biblical Witness

What is the biblical witness for persecution and suffering?

Jesus did not tell his disciples that life would be easy for believers. In fact Jesus *promised* persecution for his followers. He said that they would receive one hundredfold reimbursement of all they had left behind – homes, brothers, sisters, mothers, children and fields – to follow him but along with this would come persecutions (Mark 10:30).

Jesus told his disciples plainly, 'If they persecuted me, they will persecute you also' (John 15:20). If the disciples were to be his servants they had to expect to be treated in the same way as their master, and not be spared from suffering.

But suffering and persecution bring spiritual rewards which the world cannot understand – a foretaste of things to come. When teaching the multitudes in the Sermon on the Mount, Jesus promised, 'Blessed are those who are persecuted because of righteousness, for theirs is the kingdom of heaven' (Matt. 5:10). He continued, 'Blessed are you when people insult you, persecute you and falsely say all kind of evil against you because of me. Rejoice and be glad, because great is your reward in heaven, for in the same way they persecuted the prophets who were before you.' The key words here are 'because of righteousness' and 'because of me'. We cannot share in the spiritual rewards if we are insulted and persecuted for our own foolhardiness.

Jesus warned that persecution would come to his followers because their message would not be fully understood; some might kill them thinking they were offering a service to God (John 16:2). Jesus warned his disciples to be wary of all men because even their family and friends would betray them, and they would be handed over to local councils and flogged in the

26

synagogues. They would be brought before governors and kings, but this would be in God's purposes as they would be witnesses to the authorities and to the Gentiles (Matt. 10:17).

In his teaching concerning the signs of the end of the age, in Luke 21, Jesus says that opportunities would be opened to believers through persecution. In the sovereignty of God, he is able to turn even the evil actions of men into the service of the Kingdom.

When we look at the early Church record in Acts we see that the disciples *did* become powerful witnesses when suffering persecution, and many people became believers because of their witness.

When Peter and John were put in jail (Acts 4), this was also a time when the number of believers grew to around 5,000. The persecution that came upon the church in Judea following Stephen's martyrdom appears to have been a time of considerable growth. The Christians were dispersed throughout the land according to Acts 8, and this is the time when Luke's account changes from the *addition* to the *multiplication* of new believers.

Acts 11:19 records that at the time of the Judean persecution the Gospel spread beyond the Jewish community to the Gentiles. There is no doubt that the persecution was a major factor in driving the Christians out of Jerusalem and Judea, and thus preventing Christianity from becoming an exclusive Jewish sect. Persecution, as Jesus had foreseen, was a major force in fulfilling God's purposes of carrying the Gospel to all nations.

The word 'martyr' is derived from the Greek word '*martus*' meaning 'a witness'. It was during this period that '*martus*' took on the additional meaning of those who were willing to be 'witnesses unto death'. Today, in the West, few Christians are called upon to be witnesses unto death. We usually think of 'witnessing' as 'testifying' without any of the overtones which accompanied it in the New Testament church.

The Teaching of Jesus

Jesus taught his disciples how to react to persecution. He said, 'Pray for those who persecute you' (Matt. 5:44) so that the witness which is given glorifies God, and 'you may be sons of your Father in heaven' by loving your enemies just as God loves them. Paul's teaching was similar. 'Bless those who persecute you; bless and do not curse' (Romans 12:14).

Jesus teaches us how to be the right kind of witnesses for him. In Matthew's account twelve were sent out by Jesus and were told to expect opposition. 'When they arrest you, do not worry about what to say or how to say it. At that time you will be given what to say, for it will not be you speaking, but the Spirit of your Father speaking through you.' (Matt. 10:19-20). This promise, of course, could only hold true for those who remain close to Jesus.

The Parable of the Sower (Matt. 13, Mark 4 and Luke 8) reminds us very clearly that persecution sorts out those whose faith is deeply rooted from those who are like the seed sown upon rocky places who 'hear the word and at once receive it with joy', but who 'when trouble or persecution comes because of the word, they quickly fall away' (Mark 4:16-17).

According to the teaching of Jesus, persecution acts as a sifting process. It is similar to threshing in which the good grain is separated from the chaff and the dust is blown away by the wind.

Another biblical analogy was the refining process of precious metals in which the molten metal heated in the furnace was separated from the impurities. Malachi refers to this and sees the Lord sitting like a refiner of silver over his people, cleansing and purifying them as the dross was removed from the molten metal until the refiner could see the perfect reflection of his face in the purified surface of the metal.

28

In New Testament times the flames of persecution acted in just this way during the troubled reigns of Nero and Domitian when many believers were brutally murdered because they refused to renounce their faith in the Lord Jesus by making the statutory declaration, 'Jesus be cursed'.

Peter in his first Epistle refers to this refining process of faith as 'of greater worth than gold, which perishes even though refined by fire'. Suffering has come 'so that your faith may be proved genuine and may result in praise, glory and honour when Jesus Christ is revealed' (1 Peter 1:7).

The Teaching of the Epistle

There are many references to persecution, suffering and trials in Paul's teaching. In his Second Letter to Timothy he says, 'Everyone who wants to live a godly life in Christ Jesus will be persecuted' (3:12). This was Paul's personal experience and he did not only endure persecution (1 Cor. 4:12) but saw it to be desirable. He believed that if we are the children and heirs of God, and thus co-heirs with Christ, then we share in his suffering in order that we may also share in his glory (Romans 8:17).

James also saw the great joy which could come from persecution – 'Consider it pure joy, my brothers, whenever you face trials of many kinds, because you know that the testing of your faith develops perseverance. . . . Blessed is the man who perseveres under trial, because when he has stood the test, he will receive the crown of life that God has promised to those who love him' (James 1:2,3 and 12).

Paul expressed the desire, 'I want to know Christ and the power of his resurrection and the fellowship of sharing in his sufferings, becoming like him in his death, and so, somehow, to attain to the resurrection from the dead' (Phil. 3:10). This has been the desire of many Christians throughout history, and the knowledge that we are able to participate in the sufferings of Christ should cause rejoicing and not occasion surprise at our being put through a painful trial (1 Peter 4:12).

To be a Christian is a privilege, 'for it has been granted to you on behalf of Christ, not only to believe in him, but also to suffer for him' (Phil. 1:29). The Apostles in the early church, after being flogged by the Sanhedrin, rejoiced 'because they had been found worthy of suffering disgrace for the Name' (Acts 5:41).

Paul in 2 Corinthians actually 'delights for Christ's sake' in weaknesses, insults, hardships, persecutions and difficulties, because 'Christ's power is made perfect in my weakness' (12:10). Paul boasted about the perseverance and faith he saw in others (2 Thess. 1:4), and kept telling the Thessalonians that they would be persecuted (1 Thess. 3:4). But persecution does not mean that we give up and retreat hurt – that would be the world's way. God's all-surpassing power enables us to be 'hard pressed on every side, but not crushed; perplexed, but not in despair; persecuted, but not abandoned; struck down, but not destroyed' (2 Cor. 4:7-9).

When persecution comes because of the Gospel, the Christian is not in the battle alone – 'Who shall separate us from the love of Christ? Shall trouble or hardship or persecution or famine or nakedness or danger or sword? . . . No, in all things we are more than conquerors through him who loved us' (Romans 8:35).

James drew an example from all the prophets who had shown patience in the face of suffering (James 5:10). In Hebrews, we hear that 'although Jesus was a son he learned obedience from what he suffered' (5:8).

We should never be ashamed of testifying to the Gospel of our Lord Jesus Christ, or ashamed of anyone who is suffering persecution (2 Tim. 1:8).

Hebrews reminds us on two occasions of our need to identify with those who are suffering persecution

(Hebrews 10:33–34 and 13:3). We need not only to pray for our suffering brothers but also both to sympathise and to empathise with them in their suffering.

We should expect the Gospel to offend when it is in contrast to, or in opposition to, worldly things. 'Woe to you when all men speak well of you.' Jesus knew that this was the ultimate compromise with the world.

Christians should expect persecution in an imperfect world when they stand up and speak the truth as God has given it in his word. We are not expected to run away but should use the suffering we experience to glorify God.

Any believer may be subjected to persecution at any time. The persecution may be a time of trial, and the New Testament provides us with guidelines on how we should react.

1 Peter 3:19 tells us that it is commendable to bear up under the pain of unjust suffering because we are conscious of God, and if we suffer according to God's will we should commit ourselves to our faithful Creator and continue to do good (1 Peter 4:19). He says, 'The God of all grace, who called you to his eternal glory in Christ, after you have suffered a little while, will himself restore you and make you strong, firm and steadfast' (1 Peter 5:10). It was through standing firm in a time of persecution that the Church at Smyrna was promised, 'Be faithful, even to the point of death, and I will give you the crown of life' (Rev. 2:10).

Underlying Principles

There are a number of principles underlying persecution which Christians in the West can learn from those who have experienced persecution or are enduring persecution today. Three outstanding principles are apparent in the lives of those suffering persecution.

They are *faith, commitment* and *simplicity of lifestyle*.

'Now faith is being sure of what we hope for, and certain of what we do not see' (Heb. 11:1). This is the confidence of those who faithfully endure persecution. Their *faith* in God makes them sure of what they hope for, and certain that a crown of righteousness is awaiting them if they are faithful to the end. Their confidence is in God, and in the promise of Jesus to be with his disciples for ever and in all circumstances. It was through faith in God that men and women in biblical times 'shut the mouths of lions, quenched the fury of flames... were tortured, and refused to be released, so that they might gain a better resurrection' (Heb. 11:33-35). Their faith enabled them to face the worst that men could do to them because their hope was set upon eternal things. They were 'looking forward to the city with foundations, whose architect and builder is God' (Heb. 11:10). This expresses the confidence of those who do not weaken even under persecution because their faith is in spiritual things that are eternal, and not in the changing values of the world.

Perhaps the most obvious principle in western eyes is *commitment*. The fact that 'Jesus is Lord' is the most important thing in a persecuted Christian's life. His commitment to Christ and his willingness to be all that Christ wants him to be, transcends everything else. In life or in death his first and absolute loyalty is to God. Nothing induces him to betray Christ; not hardship nor ridicule; not suffering nor imprisonment; not even torture nor death. The true Christian counts it a privilege to suffer for the sake of the Gospel and to share in the fellowship of Christ's suffering. His commitment to Christ is total.

Another underlying principle relates to *lifestyle*. Those who are experiencing persecution simplify their lifestyle so that they are not carrying any unnecessary baggage or weight that might hinder them in what they are called by God to do and to be. They have discovered that which is really essential to them, and are able to hold lightly to the unimportant.

Material possessions mean little to those who have put Christ first and foremost in their lives and are prepared to die for their faith. It is, perhaps, not until persecution comes that Christians really face the cost of discipleship. Jesus never said that discipleship would be easy; in fact, he said that the true disciple must be prepared to renounce his own life. 'Anyone who does not carry his cross and follow me cannot be my disciple . . . in the same way, any of you who does not give up everything he has cannot be my disciple' (Luke 14:26–33).

Questions

1 Paul said 'Everyone who wants to live a godly life in Christ Jesus will be persecuted' (2 Tim. 3:12). Do you agree with this? Is it too easy to be a Christian in the West? Can we grow strong in faith without trials and tribulations? In what sense does faith in God provide the Christian with a protective covering from difficulties in the world?

2 Persecution can come from secular or religious sources. Could persecution occur today in western nations? What forms would it take? What makes Christians persecute other Christians? Is it happening today?

3 Can freedom and tolerance which are highly valued in the West co-exist with religious fanaticism? Should persecution be avoided at all costs? Does anybody court persecution and bring it on themselves? Does our toleration encourage others to be tolerant of us?

4 Are there ways in which we can help those who are facing persecution – in our own country or in other countries? We can pray – but what else should we be doing?

5 Does God allow us to suffer persecution in order to work out his purposes? Can these be achieved without persecution?

6 Why is there a link between persecution and the growth of the Church?

7 Seeing what has happened to the nations of Europe, is it really a good thing for a nation to become a Christian country? Can Church and government be closely linked? How long can the Church remain pure without experiencing persecution?

8 The three underlying principles noted in this chapter were 'faith', 'commitment' and lifestyle'. Can you add others which are relevant to the Church in the West?

Chapter Three

Shaking and Revival

I will shake all nations, and the desired of all nations will come, and I will fill this house with glory, says the Lord Almighty.

Haggai 2:7

Rich Christians

Strictly speaking, 'revival' is a fresh turning to God by those who have known him and have turned away, whereas a 'spiritual awakening' is a movement which brings multitudes of first-time believers into the Kingdom. There is a strong link between revivals and spiritual awakenings because the latter often start with a revival among Christians, and then spread to those who have no Christian background and no prior knowledge of the Gospel. China is a good example of this. The spiritual awakening sweeping across China today began with a revival of faith among the tiny Christian minority who survived the years of Communist persecution. Similarly, in Indonesia, the present spiritual awakening which is reaching Muslims and Animists began with revival among the Christians.

There are other factors also that appear to create the conditions in which revivals and spiritual awakenings flourish. A major factor is what we may term 'the shaking of a nation'. Time after time we discover that the nations in which revivals have occurred were suffering some great social, political or economic upheaval.

Indonesia

The revival in Indonesia in 1965 not only followed a year of famine, but also coincided with an unsuccessful Communist coup which proved to be one of the bloodiest periods in the history of these islands. It is estimated that more than a million lost their lives as anarchy spread through the nation, but the full number of dead will never be known.

The whole nation of Indonesia was being shaken when the revival started. It began among simple, unlearned peasant farmers on the far eastern island of Timur, and spread through the other islands like a prairie fire, providing a positive alternative to the instability that was all around.

The ground had been prepared by a healing campaign of J. Ratuwulu, and by a team visit to Soe in July 1965 under Detmar Scheunemann. But when a local teacher, Hennie Tunli'u, had a vision, which she shared at a youth rally, over 100 young people went forward and formed the basis of teams which moved across the island and then across the nation. The revival started as a lay movement based on visions and dreams, prophecy, miracles and the public confession of sin. There were many manifestations of the power of Christ to heal and to transform lives. Signs and wonders were performed through simple believers, who had a confident expectation in the power of the name of Jesus and used the gifts of the Holy Spirit which had been bestowed upon them.

An outline of the events of that time has been recorded in a number of books, including Mel Tari's *Like a Mighty Wind*.

Indonesia has a long history of colonial domination. Many of the 13,677 islands lying off the north coast of Australia that make up the present nation, were originally Dutch colonies. During the Second World War, the islands were occupied by the Japanese, and there was considerable suffering. When Japan was defeated in 1945, the people seized the opportunity to throw off all allegiance to foreign domination. Independence Day was declared on 17 August 1945, and many stone memorials exist to commemorate this date throughout the islands. A new nation was born, although the Dutch (supported by the British) fought hard for several years to try to retain their former colonies. The islands became a united entity with Jakarta, on the island of Java, as its capital. They are now the fifth most populous country in the world with a population of 165 million, two-thirds of whom live on the island of Java. It is also worth noting that more than half the population are under twenty, and have not yet reached the main child-bearing years. Thus Indonesia is preparing for an enormous population explosion during the next twenty years.

During the 1950s and 1960s, the Communist influence had increased throughout the islands, and resulted in the particularly horrific attempted coup, backed by the Chinese government. For a time, the Communist forces appeared to be winning as they took over the radio stations, and there was chaos throughout the nation. The many different national groups, who had been living peaceably together, now began to separate, and fierce inter-racial and inter-tribal conflict ensued. The great divide between rich and poor, the haves and the have-nots, also erupted in the conflict. A general atmosphere of mistrust and hatred swept the islands. Political anarchy, lawlessness and chaos reigned. Hundreds of thousands of innocent people were killed to settle old disputes, and to satisfy fancied wrongs. The Chinese community, in particular, suffered in communal massacres. Many of the survivors say that streams and rivers flowed with blood.

The government forces eventually restored order and began the task of reconstructing the nation, helped very much by the spiritual revival which had begun during those dark days. The revival helped to restore order to the nation as the love of Christ broke through the barriers of fear and mistrust, and actually united those of different tribal and communal groups, who had formerly regarded each other as enemies. The Gospel began to exercise a reconciling and healing mission in the nation. When the revival began, the total Christian presence was probably less than 10 per cent. Today, the Muslim government officially puts it as 20 per cent although it is probably much higher. Twenty-five years after the coup that shook the nation and saw the beginning of a great spiritual awakening, there are still vast numbers of new believers entering all the churches, but especially the younger indigenous churches which are springing up throughout Indonesia.

Alex Tanusaputra

Alex Tanusaputra, a businessman at the time of the coup, attended a revival meeting, and an evangelist laid hands on him, prophesying that 'within a short time you will become a servant of God'. Alex smiled to himself; he had no intention of leaving his successful business – but God had other plans for him!

Three months later when the coup was at its height, Alex had a car accident while driving at high speed. An eleven-year-old boy was terribly injured and near to death. The boy's family sought Alex out and threatened to kill him if the bleeding did not stop and their son died. Alex knew that the threat could have been carried out without difficulty in the country's current climate of chaos.

In fear, he ran to a church and prayed. He begged forgiveness for his sins and asked for the Lord's protection. He remembered the evangelist's words and offered himself as a servant of God if his life was spared. He promised to sell his belongings and to resign from business affairs. All that night he found himself repeating, 'Alive in the name of Jesus', and praying fervently for the life of the boy. A miracle occurred the following day - the boy's bleeding stopped, and he was able to have a blood transfusion. Three weeks later he was sent home well.

Alex did not forget his promise, and thanked God for his safety and for the answered prayer. During the next five years, he devoted himself to preaching the Gospel. He sold his home and, during those years, travelled, establishing seven churches and fourteen mission posts of evangelism - as well as baptising 5,000 people!

The five years of marvellous service were followed by some testing years of poverty when he had to drive a taxi to support his family. His youngest son, who was born during this period, had reached the age of five without ever having walked or talked. In 1976, Alex was praying and studying the Scriptures when John 14:12 stood out with startling clarity. 'Anyone who has faith in me will do what I have been doing.' The promise came alive for him; he claimed it; and prayed over his son, 'walk and talk in the Name of Jesus!' The next six months saw a miracle of transformation, and the boy is now a healthy, active teenager, even able to drive a car.

With his faith renewed, Alex gave up his taxi driving, moved to Surabaya, the second largest city in the nation and a strong Muslim area, believing the Lord had told him to lay claim to a piece of land, and plant a church. He was led to a large plot of land, and daily he walked round it praying. He went to see the land's owner, who was sick. Alex prayed over him, he was miraculously healed and promptly gave the land for a church.

Alex's family of seven had already begun worshipping together as a tiny church, and, as soon as the land was given, they started to build a hall to seat 300. His faith was justified; within a year, even before it was finished, it was full. Again, he began building. This time a worship centre to seat 1,000, alongside the original hall. Three years later, in 1981, this too was full to capacity, and he began on yet another new building – to seat 5,000. The congregation began worshipping there in 1986, and it was already full to capacity before the windows were even fitted, and the earlier building was being used as a Bible school with 500 students.

At the beginning of 1987, I spoke in this church at the 6 a.m. service, which was full to overflowing. In the front rows, I counted about 70 people in white gowns, and enquired if this was a special baptismal service. Pastor Alex replied, 'Oh no, we baptise this number every Sunday morning.' When I returned in October 1988, I found the congregation had risen to 17,000, and six Sunday services were held. Pastor Alex reported that they were no longer able to baptise all the new believers on Sundays, so they were now baptising on Wednesdays as well. Plans were well in hand for a new church to seat 25,000 on another site, which would also accommodate a School of Ministry. Other buildings will provide accommodation for orphans and elderly widows, plus special facilities for praying, a retreat centre and vocational study centre.

There is an important spiritual principle that is illustrated both in the national experience of revival in Indonesia and in the personal experience of Pastor Alex Tanusaputra. It is that when our lives are radically shaken, it opens us up to fresh spiritual experiences. When a nation is shaken to its foundations there is an enormous opportunity for evangelism. When the old certainties in which people put their trust are proved to be false, they are receptive to the truth of the Gospel. This spiritual principle underlies the purposes of God in shaking the nations, and can be seen throughout the world today.

Carmel and Uganda
It was when I attended an international six-day prayer gathering in Israel that this spiritual principle

took on an even wider significance. The conference was in a remote centre on Mount Carmel in Northern Israel, and there was a sense of separation from the world which we felt was ideal for prayer and for listening to God. But suddenly, the world invaded our peace.

One of the participants was Michael Cassidy, the leader of Africa Enterprise. Within an hour of his arrival there was a telephone message to say that his close companion, the evangelist, the Rev. John Wilson, had just been murdered on the streets of Kampala. He and Bishop Festo Kivengere were preparing for a major evangelistic mission in Uganda when he was dragged from his car and shot in broad daylight in front of his wife, Mary. His assailant had robbed him and stolen the car.

Michael left almost immediately to be with Mary and the family. The event had a profound effect upon the conference. We had tried to get away from the world to listen to the voice of the Spirit, but the pressures of the world had followed us. We had to ask ourselves if, through this, God was actually saying something to us. One after another, the participants recalled how God often speaks through the shattering experiences in life. We remembered that the still, small voice that Elijah heard *followed* the storm. Maybe Elijah would not have been prepared to hear if it had not been for the awesome experience of the storm which not only shattered his peace but also shook the rocks on the mountainside.

But what of John Wilson's death – did he die in vain? Amazingly, he achieved more for the unity of the church in Uganda by his ignominious death than he might have achieved had he lived. The whole church in Uganda was shaken by this needless act of violence, and it spoke deeply to them about the state of the nation and their responsibility to declare the word of God. Leaders from many different churches came together in an unprecedented way to give thanks for

John Wilson's life and resolved to commit themselves afresh to work together to bring the nation to Christ.

China
Nowhere is the link between the shaking of a nation and spiritual awakening more clearly seen than in China. The Communist Revolution of 1949 shook the foundations of the whole social structure that had remained static for thousands of years. This was followed by the Cultural Revolution of 1966, which shook the foundations of the religious beliefs and values of the nation. The outstanding effect was to destroy the commitment of the people to ancestor worship and to Buddhism, in an attempt to eradicate religion. A whole generation of young people has grown up in China with no religion; but there can be no such thing as a spiritual vacuum. There is an innate hunger in the human heart for communion with God – or at least with some supernatural power. A spiritual vacuum is quickly filled either with the false or the true knowledge of God. In China, it has given birth to the greatest spiritual awakening of the century with millions turning to Christ every year.

The events in China also illustrate the sovereignty of God over the nations. Just as God used Cyrus (Isaiah 45), the pagan Persian king who did not even know the name of God, to carry out his purposes, so in China he used those who were the enemies of Christ to prepare the way for the Gospel.

Following the Communist Revolution, all Western missionaries were expelled from China, the churches were closed, and pastors were executed or imprisoned. Bibles were burnt and the Bible colleges were closed. This was part of a much greater purge of all Western influence, and a deliberate attempt to break down the old feudal system. The aim was to create an egalitarian socialist society. Western missionaries had been operating in China for more than 100 years, and those there in 1949 feared that the Revolution would mark the end of the church. In fact, it was the beginning of a new and vibrant church in China. No one could foresee how God would use the violent upheavals in China to work out his purposes there. The missionaries' work had been hard, and there was not much fruit to show – probably less than a million believers in the whole of China. But the seed had been sown even though the door to the West was now closed.

It is estimated that Christians now number at least 50 million and possibly 100 million with approximately ten million new believers being added to the church every year. Jonathon Chao, the director of the Chinese Church Research Centre in Hong Kong, sees three major factors that account for the phenomenal growth of the church in China.

1. He speaks of the cleansing effect of the persecution that purged the church of half-hearted believers. Those whose faith survived the flames of persecution were on fire for the Lord Jesus; nothing could stop them sharing their faith even when times were bad, so that when the restrictions were lifted they were ready for every opportunity.
2. Dr Chao speaks of the spiritual vacuum left by the Cultural Revolution, and the great hunger in people's hearts that the Gospel was able to fill.
3. He refers to the growing army of travelling evangelists that has spontaneously arisen in China. It is led by those who have survived the trials of persecution, but the bulk of the army is young people whose confidence is in the Lord Jesus, and who travel from village to village and town to town sharing Christ everywhere they go.

Thousands of new churches are being planted across the length and breadth of China, usually starting in the homes of ordinary believers. The Church in China is no longer a Western institution, in its new indigenous form it is meeting the spiritual needs of the Chinese people.

The nation, which has experienced the greatest political and cultural upheavals in modern times, is now experiencing the greatest growth-rate of the Church in the world. The shaking of the nation became the birth pangs of new spiritual life.

Poor Christians

The situation in the western world some twenty or thirty years ago was very different from today. At that time there appeared to be little shaking of the western nations; they appeared to be in control of the world with everything going right for them, and seemed all set to continue to lead the world in technological development and economic power and wealth. Even the church basked in western affluence and the confidence of an unchanging world. There was little concept of the revolutionary changes that were about to break, or even of the necessity for change.

Britain, like most European nations, was considered to be a Christian country. Even though there was a falling away of the numbers attending church, this could be accounted for quite rationally by the increased mobility of people and the greater use of leisure facilities. It was recognised that there was a need for families to spend time relaxing together at weekends. Television was now in every home, but was not seen as a threat to family life and morality even though it took up ever-increasing time; time which had previously been devoted to building relationships through the church.

Few people perceived the significance of the revolutionary social changes that were occurring in Britain. The decline in the number of children attending Sunday School was seen as a natural process due to the lowering age of maturation and of the age at which children take personal responsibility for their lives. The church attempted to bridge the gap between Sunday School and church by introducing Junior Church so that families could attend morning worship together, instead of relying on parents sending their children to afternoon Sunday School. The lack of children in the church was seen as part of a natural process – the rebellion of youth – but it was expected that they would come back as they matured and settled down; they would bring their children with them, and the church would continue as a strong pillar of society. The church still appeared well respected and secure in its position in the nation. There was no great cause for concern. Radical change was not anticipated.

During the period of affluence that embraced the whole western world and lasted for two or three decades, many changes did take place. It was a period when the forces of secular humanism made great inroads into society and led to revolutionary changes in the law that reflected the permissiveness of the 'swinging sixties' when anything and everything was permitted and even encouraged. Laws based upon Christian principles that upheld social stability and public morality were questioned by those who saw no need for a faith, and many were revoked as irrelevant in a modern society which had no need of God. Still the church did not respond or even appear to notice what was happening. Major changes in legislation took place on marriage and divorce, homosexual behaviour, abortion, censorship, race relationships and sexual equality. This was the period when the right of the freedom of the individual to do whatever he wanted took over from doing what God wanted.

The phrase coined by Prime Minister Harold Macmillan, 'You've never had it so good', became the catchword of the era and marked a high point in the nation's success in worldly terms. This was the time when we learnt to put our trust in ourselves; when we believed that we could do anything in our world – the economy was booming, unemployment was low, we were unaware of the many social problems seething beneath the surface in our cities at home while overseas we were divesting ourselves of our responsibilities for the Commonwealth with comparative ease. As we took more and more power to control our world on our own, and pushed God into the background, we were oblivious of the time-bomb we were creating for ourselves for the future. It was primed to explode in the 1980s.

There is an old Danish parable that is applicable to Britain's situation. It concerns a spider who had built his web in the doorway of a large barn. He caught many flies and never had to worry about food. He grew fat and lazy and took his affluence as the rightful reward of his labour. He took to travelling around his domain admiring the fruits of his handiwork and congratulating himself on how well he had done. On one such tour, the sunlight reflected a single strand leading from the web and going high into the rafters. It offended his eye, so he broke it off – and his whole world collapsed!

Shaking

Today, Britain has lost the confidence of the 1960s and 1970s. The buoyant economy has disappeared; industrial and social problems have flooded in, together with high unemployment and low standards of personal and public morality. A high rate of marriage breakdown has weakened family life and contributed to child abuse. Crime rates have been rising steadily for a decade, and violence has become a familiar characteristic of city life. The violent behaviour of British football hooligans at European matches brought shame upon the whole nation, and this violence has also spread to Spanish holiday resorts.

The widening gap between rich and poor has

increased industrial and social unrest and created a division between the north and south of the country. Social and economic problems have been compounded by increasing anxiety over the environment, and the realisation of the serious consequences of the pollution of the air, the land, the rivers and the sea, which has resulted from our reckless exploitation of natural resources and relentless pursuit of wealth.

The nation is being shaken by the multitude and magnitude of the problems we are encountering. But this shaking is having the effect of creating a new openness to religion. Our confidence in the ability of science and technology to solve all problems has been shattered. People are now more open to what God has to say than when everything was going smoothly and well. They are turning to religion for answers to the questions they are unable to answer themselves.

Very few, however, are naturally turning to Christ because for a whole generation there has been a lack of biblical teaching, and there is, therefore, a woeful ignorance of the Gospel. The churches, moreover, do not have a good image in Britain. The disunity and uncertainty of the churches does not inspire confidence that they have the answers to the problems. Even if they did have the answers, the churches appear powerless to communicate with the people.

It is often said that mankind is incurably religious. There is evidence to support this in the present state of post-Christian Britain. Most people hold to a kind of folk religion or some kind of vaguely religious superstition. The first thing that many people read in the daily newspapers is the horoscopes. Books on occultism and witchcraft are widely read and occult films are very popular. There is considerable interest in Eastern mysticism; the cults are attracting many who are seeking spiritual enlightenment, and both Islam and Buddhism have increasing numbers of followers in Britain today.

Despite the spiritual hunger evident among the masses, many Christians seem unaware of the opportunities and are reluctant to share their faith. The majority of churches still appear to be paralysed by the old 'failure' syndrome, and are therefore slow to respond to the new openness in the nation to the Gospel.

This same story could be repeated all over Europe, although in many ways Britain seems to be more conscious of the state of decline than some other nations. Those nations which were once spiritually rich, and were most active in overseas missions, taking the Gospel to 'the ends of the earth', appear today to be largely spiritually bankrupt. Europe has now come to be known as the most secular continent in the world. In less than a century, it has sunk from being the most Christian continent to being the least Christian, although remnants of the faith can still be seen in many areas of national life. Many Europeans would still call themselves Christians, although they would not see the necessity of attending church or committing themselves, in any significant way, to an active Christian life.

Historical Perspectives

The examples given in the preceding sections have shown a link between the shaking of a nation and spiritual movements. China is an outstanding example of a nation where the radical shaking of the social and cultural systems has contributed to the present spiritual awakening that is sweeping the nation. Similarly, in Indonesia the time of social upheaval and anarchy following an attempted Communist coup prepared the ground for revival in the churches and the spiritual awakening. Other examples could also have been given, such as South Korea where the ruinous civil war of the 1950s prepared the way for spiritual awakening. In thirty years the Christian community in South Korea has grown from a mere 5 per cent to more than 30 per cent of the total population.

Ready for Revival
In Britain, historians have noted the link between sociopolitical conditions and spiritual revival. The Wesleyan Revival of the eighteenth century coincided with a period of mounting unrest among working-class people because of poor social conditions, poverty and oppression by the rich. The Industrial Revolution that had drawn workers from rural communities into the new industrial centres of population, created a new class of landless peasants. Their condition was worse than that of their country cousins, who at least were able to grow food to enable them to survive. The Industrial Revolution not only created the landless poor, but also created a new middle-class from among the rising bourgeoisie of industrialists and merchants. Basic changes in the structure of society began to take place at this time. For centuries, ownership of land had been the primary source of wealth and power in Britain. The new source of wealth lay in industrial production. Thus, every sector of society in Britain was being shaken by fundamental changes. The old order of life was beginning to crumble. As the old certainties upon which people had put their trust began to disappear, the conditions for revival were created.

Wesley's emphasis upon the need for conversion as a personal experience of God, and forgiveness of sin leading to a total moral and spiritual change, came as good news to the poor. It brought them the assurance of God's love for each individual, who mattered sufficiently for Christ to die for them. It gave them a new status as sons of God in a society where status was denied them.

Wesley's preaching, however, did not come as good news to the established Church where rationalism, intellectualism and close identification with the privileged social class made it closed to any fresh spiritual experience, which was despised as emotionalism.

Nevertheless, the Wesleyan Revival did reach beyond the communities of the poor. It reached many in the new middle-classes and those who enjoyed positions of social privilege, who were shaken by events across the Channel where the French Revolution had created a reign of terror. There was great fear among the rich and privileged in Britain that similar things might happen here.

Many historians agree that it was the revival led by Wesley and Whitefield that saved England from the horrors of revolution similar to the French. When revival sweeps a nation it brings radical changes to its moral and spiritual life that can actually change the course of history.

The Welsh Revival at the beginning of the twentieth century was born under similar social conditions. Life was very hard in the Welsh valleys at that time, unemployment was rising and there was grinding poverty. But the Welsh sang praises to God as they faced their physical problems with spiritual strength. The Welsh revival is notable in that it was largely confined to the poor mining communities labouring under the oppression of the rich. The revival did not touch those who were more privileged, and were unaware of their spiritual needs.

Similarly, at the birth of the Pentecostal movement in the 1920s, it was the poor and the underprivileged members of society who responded. It was not until the Second World War had shaken the confidence of the nation, the loss of Empire and diminishing prosperity of the 1970s that the middle-classes in Britain were open to receiving the new life of the Spirit.

There is strong evidence for a link between the shaking of a nation's self-confidence and openness to moral and spiritual reform. When a nation places all its trust in material prosperity or political and military power, so long as it is successful, its people will be closed to spiritual values. But this opens the door to corruption and the decay of moral values, which in turn leads to the undermining of the social and political structure of society. It is at this point that openness to reform comes. In God's perfect timing a new movement of the Spirit begins in the hearts of those who have remained faithful to the truth of the Gospel. It brings revival and fresh confidence to the believers and soon spills over into the secular community and may then spread like a prairie fire across the nation in revivals and spiritual awakenings.

Under the sovereignty of God, the shaking of a nation that appears to be a day of disaster is transformed into the day that brings hope and a new future. The old has to fall away before the new can be born. It is the spiritual principle of death and resurrection. The old corrupt body of death must be buried for the new to come fully to life.

Biblical Witness

We noted earlier in this chapter that revival is a term that applies to a period when a Christian community experiences a renewal of faith, and that the term spiritual awakening is a term that should be used when the movement brings into faith large numbers of those who had no previous background of faith. Throughout the Bible there are numerous examples of periods of spiritual growth. Strictly speaking, those that occurred in Old Testament times were revivals, whereas those that occurred in New Testament times, particularly when the Gospel began to break new ground into the Gentile world, were spiritual awakenings.

The Children of Israel

Tracing the spiritual health of Israel through the centuries is rather like riding a roller coaster. This is neatly summarised in the complaint that God brings against the Israelites through the prophet Hosea. 'When I fed them, they were satisfied; when they were satisfied, they became proud; then they forgot me' (Hosea 13:6).

The major task of the prophets was to warn the nation when they saw it drifting into apostasy, and to call the people back to faithfulness to God. The prophets perceived the danger facing the nation that turned away from God, a turning away from truth into error, that could only lead to national disaster. It was for this reason that the prophets saw themselves as the watchmen of the nation. Hosea expressed this as, 'the prophet, along with my God, is the watchman over Ephraim' (Hosea 9:8), and Ezekiel saw this as his major calling. 'Son of man, I have made you a watchman for the house of Israel; so hear the word I speak and give them warning from me' (Ezekiel 33:7).

The warnings given by the prophets usually included an interpretation of contemporary events showing why everything was going wrong in the life of the nation. Jeremiah explained why the spring rains had not fallen to ensure a good harvest – 'Your wrong doings have kept these away; your sins have deprived you of good' (Jeremiah 5:25). Amos catalogued the disasters of his day with the refrain after each event, 'yet you have not returned to me, says the Lord' (Amos 4:6–12). The great desire of the prophets was to see the nation return to obedience and a right relationship with God, but they knew that this could only happen through repentance and through turning away from their evil deeds and the worship of foreign gods.

The prophets saw that the key to the spiritual health of the nation lay in repentance which, in turn, would lead not only to spiritual revival but also to the revival of the fortunes of the nation. The emphasis of the prophets was not to urge repentance in order to reap the rewards of spiritual righteousness in material prosperity, but rather that they could not conceive of God blessing a nation who had broken the terms of the Covenant with him through faithlessness. Repentance led to revival; a renewing of the spiritual life of the nation which brought them back into a right relationship with God, and to the restoration of the blessings promised in the Covenant.

Hezekiah's Revival

An outstanding example of repentance and revival occurred early in the reign of the young King Hezekiah who, at the age of 25, succeeded his father Ahaz, one of the most notorious idolaters to occupy the throne of Judah. Ahaz had set up idols in Jerusalem and shrines to foreign gods throughout the land. He had disbanded the priests and closed the Temple. All this occurred at a time of great threat to the security of the nation from the rising power of the Assyrian empire. The northern kingdom of Israel had already fallen, and it was clear that the tiny nation of Judah would soon suffer the same fate.

Hezekiah's first act in the first month of his reign was to re-open the Temple and to bring the priests back to Jerusalem to reconsecrate themselves and the Temple. He removed all traces of idolatry from the Temple and re-established worship. Then he summoned the whole nation to a celebration of the Passover in Jerusalem. He even sent letters inviting the people of Israel, who were living under Assyrian rule, to come and join their brethren in a united act of worship. Israel had been separated from Judah for about 200 years and there was considerable hostility between the tribes. Some of them scorned the invitation and ridiculed, but, nevertheless, others humbled themselves and went to Jerusalem (2 Chron. 30:11), and 'a very

53

large crowd of people assembled in Jerusalem to celebrate the Feast of Unleavened Bread in the second month. They removed the altars in Jerusalem and cleared away the incense altars and threw them into the Kidron valley' (2 Chron. 30:13-14).

Traditionally, the Passover is celebrated in the first month of the Jewish year. This break with tradition, by celebrating Passover in the second month, is an indication of the emergency facing the nation and the urgency of bringing the whole nation before God. Isaiah was the prophet during this period and no doubt his warnings and pleadings with the nation to repent had a large influence upon the actions of Hezekiah.

All those who were present in Jerusalem celebrated the Feast of Unleavened Bread with great rejoicing, and there was such enthusiasm that they simply could not stop worshipping God. The festival, therefore, was extended for seven more days and 'there was great joy in Jerusalem, for since the days of Solomon son of David king of Israel there had been nothing like this in Jerusalem' (2 Chron. 30:26). The chronicler records that the priests and Levites and the whole assembly of Judah rejoiced.

But the most significant statement is that 'all who had assembled from Israel, including the aliens' also rejoiced. The aliens were pagan communities, resettled in Israel by the Assyrians. They would not, of course, be allowed into the Temple but the revival fervour overflowed from the Temple worshippers into the outer courts of the Gentiles, and into the streets of Jerusalem so that the whole city was filled with joy. That is what happens in a revival – even the unbelievers get caught up in it, and fresh spiritual life flows throughout the nation. Revival is the fruit of repentance; the blessing that is poured out upon a nation that humbly returns to its God.

In Hezekiah's revival the entire assembly then went out through the towns of Judah smashing the sacred stones and cutting down the Asherah poles, the symbols of the apostasy from which they had turned away. They demonstrated their new-found faith in God by cleansing the land of idolatry.

But the revival that took place at this time did not ensure for them a peaceful future – in fact it was a preparation for a further time of shaking and it provided them with the strength they needed to come through the testing days ahead. The Assyrian onslaught upon Judah was not long delayed. The revival not only gave them the spiritual power to stand against the enemy, but the faith to believe that God would give them the victory. The historical record concludes, 'King Hezekiah and the prophet Isaiah, son of Amoz, cried out in prayer to heaven about this. And the Lord sent an angel, who annihilated all the fighting men and the leaders and officers in the camp of the Assyrian king. So he withdrew to his own land in disgrace' (2 Chron. 32:20–21).

The events in the time of Hezekiah are an illustration of a basic spiritual principle that is found in the prophecy of Haggai 2:6 and 7. 'In a little while I will once more shake the heavens and the earth, the sea and the dry land. I will shake all nations, and the desired of all nations will come, and I will fill this house with glory, says the Lord Almighty.' It is clearly stated here that there is a link between the shaking of the nations and the time of spiritual harvest.

A fuller interpretation of this principle is found in Hebrews 12:26 to 29 where the prophecy of Haggai is repeated. Here it is stated that created things will be shaken, that is, the whole materialistic order of creation, 'so that what cannot be shaken may remain'. The thing that cannot be shaken is the Kingdom. Thus it is God's intention to use the shaking of the nations and the realm of nature to bring forth the Kingdom. 'Therefore, since we are receiving a kingdom that cannot be shaken, let us be thankful, and so worship God acceptably with reverence and awe, for our God is a consuming fire.'

The Steadfast God

There are numerous references throughout the Bible to the whole natural order of creation being shaken, but continually the Lord reassures those who love him and are faithful to his word, that they will not be shaken. David had this confidence in the Lord. He said, 'because he (God) is at my right hand, I will not be shaken' (Psalm 16:8). He also declared, 'He alone is my rock and my salvation; he is my fortress, I shall never be shaken' (Psalm 62:2).

It was because of God's great love for his people that they could have such confidence in him. This is beautifully expressed in Isaiah 54:10 – 'Though the mountains be shaken and the hills be removed, yet my unfailing love for you will not be shaken nor my covenant of peace be removed, says the Lord, who has compassion on you.'

God's purpose in shaking the nations and the whole of natural creation is to shake man's confidence in material things and in his own ability to rule the world. His intention is to open up mankind to the Gospel as the only power to bring man into a right relationship with God, and to bring peace and harmony to the whole order of creation.

The spiritual awakenings that we see following the shaking of the nations today may be regarded as a shadow of the great harvest of the Kingdom that Scripture declares will occur in the end times. The final shaking of all things will be a prelude to the fulfilment of the promise that the day will come when 'at the name of Jesus every knee should bow, in heaven and on earth and under the earth, and every tongue confess that Jesus Christ is Lord, to the glory of God the Father' (Phil. 2:10–11).

Underlying Principles

There are several basic principles that can be discerned from the accounts of revivals that have coincided with periods of social and political upheaval or the 'shaking' of nations. Two such principles have particular relevance for our consideration. They are *trust in God* and *openness to change*.

It was the Psalmist's great *trust in God* that gave him the confidence to declare 'we will not fear, though the earth give way and the mountains fall into the heart of the sea' (Psalm 46:2). In the same way, it was Paul's trust in God that enabled him to declare that 'nothing in all creation will be able to separate us from the love of God which is in Christ Jesus our Lord' (Romans 8:39). This absolute trust in God is to be seen in all the great servants of the Lord whose confidence was not placed in material things but in the unchanging nature of God and his great love for us. Those who trust in the Lord know that he has good plans for our lives, in Jeremiah's words 'plans to prosper you and not to harm you, plans to give you hope and a future' (Jeremiah 29:11).

This same confidence can be ours today even when our personal lives are being shaken or when the nation of which we are a part is going through a period of turmoil.

The prophets continually appealed to the people to be *open to change* their ways, to turn away from evil and to put their trust in God. Jeremiah stated explicitly that the blessings of God could only come upon a nation in a right relationship with God. He said, 'If you really change your ways and your actions and deal with each other justly . . . then I will let you live in this place . . . declares the Lord' (Jeremiah 7:5–11).

Jesus also spoke of the necessity for radical change. He said, 'I tell you the truth, unless you change and become like little children, you will never enter the kingdom of heaven' (Matt. 18:3).

It is surprising how often we resist change even though we are aware that it is for our good. Most men and women have a natural fear of change – we cling onto the things we know even though they are not ideal, rather than risk something unknown. We are afraid of change because we lack trust in God.

It is here that we see the link between these two underlying principles – trust in God and openness to change. Our confidence in God creates a readiness to accept whatever the future holds because we know that God will be with us to lead, to guide, to protect and to carry us through any period of change however threatening it may appear. When we have a confidence in the sovereignty of God we are able to face the future knowing that he is in control and that he is working out his purposes which are ultimately for our good.

We see this confidence in all the great men and women of faith throughout Scripture. It is beautifully summarised in Hebrews 11 which begins, 'Faith is being sure of what we hope for and certain of what we do not see'. It was this confidence in God that enabled Abraham to leave his home community and set out for the Promised Land. It was this same confidence in God that inspired Henry Francis Lyte to write, 'Change and decay in all around I see, O Thou who changest not abide with me', and Paul to declare, 'We know that in all things God works for the good of those who love him' (Romans 8:28).

There are of course other underlying principles which you will be able to discover for yourselves, and which need to be applied to today's situation.

Questions
1 What are the signs that the nations are being shaken today? Is the church being shaken as well?

2 What are God's purposes in shaking the nations? Are there elements of warning, judgment, pruning, refining . . . ? Discuss in the light of Haggai 2:6 and 7 and Hebrews 12:26–29.

3 This chapter has been drawing out the links between shaking and revivals, but not all shaking leads to revival. Why not? In what ways do Christians act as a blockage to revival?

4 Times of shaking create openness to the Gospel. Do you think the church is ready to respond to the opportunities being presented today? What about your fellowship and what about you?

5 The secularisation of once-Christian nations presents particular problems for the mission of the church in communicating the Gospel. What are they and how can they be met?

6 Revival usually brings repentance to both believers and unbelievers. Does 2 Chronicles 7:14 mean that the conditions for revival can be created by the repentance of believers?

7 Revivals take many forms and although they usually start with a fresh spiritual experience among believers, the institutional church is often slow to respond. Why should this be?

8 Two basic principles of 'Trust in God' and 'Openness to Change' have been drawn out in this chapter. Are there others relating to shaking and revival which are relevant to Christians in the West?

Chapter Four

Growth in Numbers

All over the world this Gospel is bearing fruit and growing, just as it has been doing among you since the day you heard it and understood God's grace in all its truth.

Col. 1:6

Rich Christians

The church worldwide is growing at a rate never previously experienced. Christianity is now the world's largest religion. One third of the world's total population now claim to be Christian and that percentage is rising. There are now more Christians in non-western nations than in Europe and America. The nations which were the missionary sending nations of the nineteenth and early twentieth centuries could soon be at the receiving end of mission.

The Christian explosion in the 'two-thirds-world' is exciting the attention of church leaders in the West, and is hastening the day when Jesus' prophecy – that the Gospel will be preached in all nations – will be fulfilled. The developing nations with their new and vibrant faith in God and their rapidly expanding churches are coming of age and are now beginning to share in the worldwide task of spreading the good news.

The vast growth in numbers taking place in some countries calls for an examination of those areas and the reasons for the growth. It is these churches that will be leading the evangelisation of the world into the twenty-first century as the church expands and the Gospel spreads. There is much that can already be learnt from these nations. First, however, it is necessary to note certain basic characteristics of numerical growth.

Components of Growth and Decline

David Barratt, editor of the *World Christian Encyclopedia*, updates the statistics each year to show the numbers of Christians in each country, denominational affiliations and many aspects of Christian demography. He lists three major factors affecting growth, and three affecting decline. He balances natural increase with death rates; immigration with emigration; and conversion with apostasy. To the last group we, in our western civilisation, need to add 'restoration of the lapsed' as a balance to the falling away of Christians. Each of these takes place in varying proportions in each country on each continent.

a) Natural increase through a high birthrate, and the lowering of the death rate is a major population factor in regions such as Africa and South America. Kenya has the highest birthrate in the world, and this produces a significant growth in the Christian community through children born into Christian families. But the church in Kenya is also growing through conversion and is currently reckoned to have the highest percentage of Christians of any African nation; 73 per cent of the Kenyan population claim to be Christian as against 65 per cent ten years ago.

But death by war, or civil war, can also reduce the size of the Christian community. At least 300,000 Christians were murdered by Idi Amin during his reign of terror in Uganda, but still the church grew during that time at a rate faster than that of the population.

b) Ease of communications and travel are making the world a smaller place. Mass immigration and emigration, which is a characteristic of our age, also affects the growth or decline of the church in an area. Australia has a Christian heritage because of emigration from Britain; in the same way the United States has strong Christian foundations because of emigration from Europe. In recent times the large-scale influx of Mexicans into the south-west of the United States has increased the Roman Catholic church there.

Nearer home, the immigration of West Indians into Britain in the 1950s and 1960s brought many more Christians to our shores. On the other hand, the immigration of Indians and Pakistanis which followed, brought many Hindus, Sikhs and Muslims into Britain, and they have established their religious communities. From another standpoint, it could be said that the 'mission field' had come to the United Kingdom.

The churches in Hong Kong have received a significant boost by the numbers of Filippinos arriving on the island to take up work permits. There has been talk of bringing a Filippino pastor over to minister to them and meet their pastoral needs, but this will almost inevitably result in a new ethnic church being planted and the withdrawal of a growth factor from the more traditional churches. This, coupled with the withdrawal of expatriates, both missionary and secular, from Hong Kong as 1997 draws nearer, indicates considerable future changes in the island's Christian scene.

Emigration dramatically affected the composition of the different religious communities in Algeria which once had a thriving Roman Catholic population among the Berbers. When the French withdrew from the country so did many of the Christians, who settled in Paris and Marseilles. Because of this the present Catholic population in Algeria is less than 1 per cent, with the Protestant community even smaller. These are just a few examples of the way in which the movement of population affects the church in different areas of the world.

c) Conversion is the main means by which the true expansion of the church can be measured, and the only one which will change the *proportions* of Christians to non-Christians worldwide. Natural increase, through children born into Christian families, hardly affects the proportion of Christians to non-Christians since the adherents of other religions are also increasing at a similar rate. Conversion from non-Christian religions and from secular atheism is taking place on a large scale in regions such as South East Asia and Indonesia, the Philippines, Malaysia, Singapore, South Korea, and also in Communist countries, such as China and the Soviet Union. There is also a high rate of conversion in many parts of Central and Southern Africa.

In stark contrast, apostasy is prevalent in many European countries, although this has been disguised somewhat because many people call themselves Christians without ever having had a conversion experience or committing their lives to Christ, and without attending church regularly. A major target of the Western church should be to restore to full faith those who have had a faith, which has now become nominal, before they take the next step and reject the Gospel completely as irrelevant. This will be referred to in greater depth in the next section.

Westernisation and after
The missionary movement which took the Gospel from Europe to other parts of the world, from the eighteenth century onwards, was closely linked with colonial expansion and westernisation. The American counterpart was not so closely associated with colonialism but it certainly had strong links with westernisation. All the western churches have tended to carry the Gospel prepackaged in western culture. In church growth terms, the missionaries have taken the plant pot as well as the plant when carrying the Gospel overseas. The new churches the missionaries planted

63

were in the same mould as those they left behind in their home countries. Even the buildings they erected took on the same shape, and the worship followed the same pattern.

Even more significantly, the mission churches looked to Europe and America not only for support but also for leadership. Mission churches until the middle of the twentieth century were led by missionaries.

The movement for independence among nations under western colonial governments, that exploded onto the world scene in the middle of the twentieth century in the immediate aftermath of the Second World War, brought about fundamental changes to the mission-church scene. Powerful political forces were at work demanding the right of nations to self-government. A wave of nationalist sentiment swept through many nations as the people sought to throw off what they saw as colonial oppression.

Many of the newly independent nations, which were formed during the 1950s and 1960s, imposed restrictions upon the length of stay of foreign nationals. This forced the churches to reconsider their whole attitude towards leadership and to advance the priority of training programmes for local leaders.

The changeover to indigenous leadership, which also began in the middle of the twentieth century, coincided with the first major wave of the Pentecostal missionary movement. The Pentecostal churches that had become firmly established in America and Britain during the 1920s and 1930s began looking overseas after the Second World War for new fields of evangelism. Their presentation of the Gospel found a ready response among people in the newly independent nations. The emphasis of the new pentecostal evangelism was upon the power of the Holy Spirit which was available to all believers. This contrasted strongly with the presentation of the Gospel by tradítional western missionaries from the mainline churches with their academic qualifications and emphasis upon the necessity of sound theological learning and western-style leadership.

Pentecostal teaching also emphasised the availability of spiritual gifts to all Christians, and this appealed strongly to the new believers in the new nations, who were discovering a new identity. Each one could play an active role in the new churches; each had something to offer as well as something to receive, and this contributed to the establishment of vibrant Christian communities. The new believers were filled with spiritual enthusiasm and could not help sharing their faith. They thus became strongly evangelising churches reflecting the local culture and presenting the Gospel in the local language. The indigenisation of the Gospel was given further impetus by the Pentecostal stress upon the power of the Holy Spirit, which led to signs and wonders, a visible demonstration of the power of the Name of Jesus to heal, to open the eyes of the blind and to make the lame walk. As in the days of Jesus, the Gospel was received as good news to the poor.

Many churches that were established by western Pentecostal preachers soon became independent as local leadership evolved and began to remould the Church into the local culture and to redirect the mission outreach according to local needs, making use of local resources. Thus it is that the indigenous churches have increasingly gained strength and spiritual power as the movement of the Spirit has gained momentum in the non-western world.

The movement of indigenisation has not only affected the new independent churches that have come out of the Pentecostal movement, but has also brought radical changes to churches that are still affiliated to the mainline western churches. This can particularly be seen in the international Anglican communion where the Bishops and other indigenous leaders from

Commonwealth countries are now taking places of leadership in what has until recently been a church very much dominated by the West.

This change was noted in an Anglican missions conference held in London in 1985. Until then 'Mother Britain' (the Church of England) had always taken the chair at all meetings and allowed discussion among her children, but the major decisions were always referred to her for her approval and consent. The British, who had never thought of it as ever being any other way, suddenly discovered that the children had grown up and were beginning to make contributions to thinking and planning and scholarship. Moreover, these contributions were being made from a point of strength; the 'children's' churches were growing whereas those of the 'parents' were suffering decline.

The experience of the Anglican church in Britain, and the realisation that her role as 'mother church' is no longer relevant, has worldwide significance and is an indicator of a major shift in the world church scene. We are going through a period in which the western churches are having to learn to receive rather than to give. It is the churches in the non-western world that are vibrant in spiritual life and experiencing rapid growth. There are many lessons that the older western churches can learn, and should be learning, from the newer non-western churches. It would be useful at this point to note some of the things that are happening in the different regions of the world, and also to note the new models that are being developed in the non-western churches.

China
China is providing us with one of the most exciting examples of conversion growth. This has already been looked at in Chapter Two as an example of the effects of persecution. The Church in Cina is growing at an incredible rate today – faster than anywhere else in

the world. But the growth actually began in the darkest days of persecution when the Bamboo Curtain was closed. China was cut off from the West and western missionaries were not available to lead or guide the church, and they are still not permitted in China today. It is estimated that the Christian presence in China is now at least 5 per cent of the total population, and in some areas it is much higher. There are reports that in one province of Northern China, 90 per cent of the population is Christian. Of course, not all are in the officially recognised 'Three Self Patriotic Churches'. These churches are also growing but so too are the so-called 'underground churches'. It is among them that, according to observers, the greatest growth is taking place.

Christians in China had to learn very quickly how to stand on their own feet if they were to survive under a communist government. The Church could no longer depend upon outside help and influence, either in leadership, resources or finance. It could not depend upon the kind of methods that it had been taught were necessary for growth, and which the Church in the West count as essential – necessities such as strong leaders, large meetings, regular services and central organisation.

In China, during this period, anybody who set themselves up as a leader soon found that they were imprisoned or executed in the hostile environment of secular atheism. Leadership had to be extremely discreet and low-key, as any known leader would be the next for the prison camps, and their witness would be restricted. Thus it was that the witness of every committed Christian became important. It was no longer possible to leave evangelism to missionaries or professional church leaders. As in the days of the early church, every believer knew themselves to be a witness for the Lord Jesus. They believed that the work of spreading the good news was so essential that it was more important than life itself.

During the latter part of the Cultural Revolution there was a significant rise in the numbers of itinerant evangelists. These were laymen, not ordained theologically trained missionaries. They were simple untrained men and women, on fire for the Lord Jesus, who gave themselves full-time to travelling from place to place preaching the Gospel in villages and small towns, wherever they could gather a small group of people. Much of this evangelism was carried out secretly in the homes of the people behind closed doors for fear of the authorities. The faith of the Christians was so strong and so contagious that they planted house churches across the length and breadth of China, and there were tiny fellowships of believers meeting in one another's houses. The church multiplied because the new believers shared the urge to communicate their faith to others. They could not keep the good news to themselves and even counted it a privilege to suffer hardship with Christ – sharing in the fellowship of his sufferings.

Large meetings were prohibited, so that all teaching of new believers had to be done in small groups. During the years in which the church was proscribed, no Sunday services could be held for worship and preaching. Instead, the Gospel had to be taken to the people in their homes. These small house fellowships laid the foundation for the mass evangelisation of China that is now taking place. The small groups not only developed personal relationships but provided the practical training ground for the new itinerant evangelists. Within the small groups, believers shared their faith with one another and recounted how the Lord protected and sustained them at work and amid all the dangers they encountered everyday.

The Christians in China had few material resources available so what little they did have was highly valued. There were so few Bibles available that single pages were often passed around from one believer to another. The Word was often learnt by heart before being passed on to someone else. The authorities could take away and destroy the printed page but the word that was planted in the hearts of the people could not be destroyed. The Christians learned to put their trust in spiritual things rather than material possessions and this created an urge to use their limited material resources in the most effective way.

Ghana

Ghana is an African nation with a long heritage of Christian mission, and of churches led by European missionaries. During the early 1970s revival swept through the land in the wake of political independence. The main characteristic of this fresh spiritual awakening was that it was a 'people movement' resulting from an 'Each One, Reach One' campaign using the multiplication principle where every believer was encouraged to bring someone to Christ. The Ghana experience proved that DIY evangelism worked. There were no mass crusades, no central organisation, simply evangelism on a one-to-one basis – believer to non-believer.

South Korea

The Korean War of the 1950s, which resulted in the division of the nation into north and south, left the whole country facing grave economic, social and political problems. The Communist north firmly shut its doors against Christianity and all other western influences, but the Christians in the south seized the opportunity to proclaim the Gospel as the only means of building a sound and secure nation. The Protestant 'work ethic' appealed strongly to the newly emerging business community in South Korea. Prosperity had to be founded upon righteousness and diligence.

In the general climate of rising prosperity and economic progress that accompanied the spiritual awakening sweeping the nation and bringing multitudes of new Christians into the Church, the conditions were created for the development of the world's largest congregations. The megachurches of South Korea are today known throughout the world, the most famous being the Full Gospel Church in Seoul, which has half a million members. There are, however, many other large churches in South Korea. It has been said, in fact, that those with under 2,000 members are scorned. South Korea not only has the largest Pentecostal church in the world, but also the largest United Methodist, the largest Presbyterian and the largest Baptist churches as well. Ten of the twenty largest churches in the world are in South Korea.

The economic prosperity at present being enjoyed by South Korea belies the political tensions that exist in the nation. These are occasionally highlighted in western news coverage of student riots as happened at the time of the 1988 Olympic Games. These tensions are a legacy from the traumas of the civil war and an indication of the frailty of the nation's existence as an independent state. A symbol of the continuing threat from North Korea is a giant dam which has been built just north of the border and which, if accidentally or intentionally released, could completely submerge Seoul in devastating flood waters.

The fear generated by this threat from the north is reflected in both the drive to carry the Gospel across the 39th Parallel into the north and also to be seen in the urgency of the prayer life of the whole Christian community in South Korea. Continuous chains of prayer are maintained with large numbers of Christians making use of 'prayer mountains'. This emphasis upon individual prayer and meditation has had its effect upon public worship. In times of open prayer in some of the large churches, the whole congregation simultaneously prays aloud in united praise or fervent intercession.

The sheer organisation and administration of such large numbers calls for management skills and creative policy thinking. The centre of Seoul on Sunday mornings is one great traffic jam with everybody trying to get to, or home from, church. Some churches have as many as ten or twelve services during the day in order to accommodate all the worshippers. This is achieved through complex transport arrangements and elaborate busing systems. Strangely, pastoral care probably takes a higher prominence than it does in many smaller churches. Additionally, a major objective of organisation is to ensure that each individual is able to play a full part in the life of the Christian community. The megachurches usually have a highly developed, three-tier system in which there are small groups for personal development, larger groups for teaching, training evangelism and social action, and mass congregations for worship and celebration events.

Nigeria

Evangelism is high on the agenda of most churches in Nigeria. The Pentecostal and independent churches are the most successful in drawing huge numbers to their meetings. As a former British colony Nigeria has a long association with western culture. Many of these influences remain today, and the official language of the state is English. Western methods are to be seen in evangelism and many famous western evangelists hold crusades in Nigeria and draw huge crowds with multitudes responding to the Gospel. Nigerian evangelists also hold mass crusades. Outstanding among the indigenous Christian leaders is Benson Idahosa of Benin City. He regularly fills the 50,000-seater football stadium to overflowing, and his larger meetings draw as many as a quarter of a million people.

But the north of Nigeria is predominantly Muslim. When the first Islamic revival in Northern Nigeria took place in 1833, there were a number there who resisted conversion to Islam, particularly around the Kaduna and Kano districts. They became known as the Maguzawa, which means those who refused or ran away. For decades, western missionaries also made little progress in introducing Christ to these strongly independent people, who lived in small, scattered communities. But a sudden change took place in the late 1970s, and since then some 6,000 people have declared their faith in Christ, resulting in some 200 churches being planted among this group alone.

Josiah Idowu, principal of an Anglican theological college, told me how the students from his college are sent out into these villages in threes each weekend to teach and worship with the growing number of Christians. Ninety-nine per cent of these people are said to be illiterate, so the Christians use the Bible to teach the language to those who cannot read. To overcome the shortage in full-time leadership in the Anglican church, two other categories have been introduced to supplement the work of ordained priests. These are the agent and the catechist or evangelist. Adult baptisms are great occasions, and when the principal went to conduct one he asked to meet the evangelists and agents in the area. To his surprise seventeen turned up. When he asked them who was their employer, they answered, 'The Lord'. When he asked who was paying them, they answered, 'The people'. They were already doing the work which the college was training people for three years to do! These people, in one year, had caught the challenge of passing on the little that had been given to them. In that area 60 new churches had been planted in five years.

Singapore
Where the church has been in existence for many years it often loses its cutting edge through tradition or complacency. When a fresh spiritual movement

takes place it often revitalises the life of the church, and brings renewal of faith to the members, which results in evangelistic outreach. This is what has happened in Singapore.

Renewal in the Anglican church began in 1972 when the Diocesan Bishop, Bishop Chiu Ban It, had a fresh experience of the Holy Spirit. The movement rapidly spread from the cathedral through all the Anglican churches on the island. Today, every Anglican congregation has experienced the renewing power of the Holy Spirit which has brought growth in all dimensions. Their training programmes are for the whole congregation and they feel very strategically placed to reach out to the whole of Asia. But it is not just the Anglican church which has experienced this renewal – it has spread through most of the churches on the island. David Barratt gives the percentage of charismatic Christians in East Asia to be 80 per cent in comparison with a worldwide 21 per cent.

No Blue-Print

The examples given above of fresh spiritual life and rapid church growth in non-Western nations reveal a number of new models from which churches in the western world can learn. They also show that there is no such thing as a standard blueprint for growth. Perhaps the overall lesson is that methods must be adapted to suit circumstances. There must be flexibility to adapt even basic principles in different cultural settings, and to meet the prevailing social and political conditions. Obviously, the Church encountering persecution has to organise its life and witness very differently from a church in an open society.

a) From the examples given above it will be seen that one-to-one *evangelism* is effective in some societies, such as Ghana and China, whereas mass evangelism is ideally suited to the situation in Nigeria. Similarly, other examples could be given where mass evangelism is bringing great fruitfulness in other parts of Africa, such as Kenya, and in many parts of Latin America.

b) Different styles of *leadership* are effective under different circumstances. South Korea provides an ideal setting for the strong, natural leader who can oversee a large pastoral team and provide a figurehead type of leadership. By contrast, leadership in China has to be very low-key and of the type that encourages whole body of Christ ministry.

c) Where the church is existing under persecution, *small groups* are essential as they are the only ones that can survive. Under other circumstances, such as an open society and a booming free-market economy, such as exists in South Korea, very *large congregations* have a strong appeal.

d) When a new movement of the Spirit takes place that extends the Church and brings in many new believers, this may result in the *planting of new churches*, as in Indonesia, or it may result in the *renewing of existing churches* as in Singapore. In those areas where the church is breaking new ground there will be a need for new fellowships, whereas in areas where the churches are well established the major emphasis may be upon renewal.

e) There is no ideal type of *organisation* that guarantees success in evangelism or in the fellowship life of the church. In fact the extreme opposites of organisation appear to be equally effective. On the one hand, in an area experiencing revival there is often an almost total lack of organisation accompanying what appears to be a kind of spontaneous explosion of spiritual energy as, for example, in Indonesia and parts of Africa. On the other hand, rapid church growth may be accompanied by a high level of organisation and efficiency as in South Korea where even the prayer life of the Christian community is well regulated.

f) Finally, it should be noted that *resources* do not guarantee success. The church that is starved of

74

material resources often thrives in its spiritual life, whereas the church that has many resources can also flourish if they are used wisely and provided that the resources do not become a substitute for dependence upon God.

Poor Christians

The Christian presence is expanding rapidly in almost every continent but, in contrast, church attendance in western Europe throughout most of this century has been witnessing a dramatic decline. Statistics of church growth and decline are notoriously difficult to interpret because of the complexity and multitude of the different factors involved. One of the greatest difficulties arises from the different ways in which the denominations enumerate their members, adherents and children. Examples are seen in some churches which include children or even baptised infants, whereas other denominations only count adult membership; some count attendance by the number of communicants at a particular annual festival, such as Easter, whereas others count only those who attend each week. Still others count all those who claim adherence, thus nominal Christians may outnumber those who are committed and active in practising their faith. The major problem facing church statisticians, therefore, is not only 'how many Christians are there?' but 'who is a Christian?'

According to David Barratt in the *Status of Global Mission*, the statistics for church *membership* in the whole of Europe (East and West) have shown an overall increase this century and continue to show a slight annual increase even today. This is accounted for by a number of factors, the most important of which is that there has been a growth in the overall population of Europe since the beginning of the twentieth century. It is church *attendance* that has suffered the greatest decline whereas nominality has increased.

For instance, in the Scandinavian countries, 97 per cent of Danes belong to the Lutheran State Church but only about 2 per cent attend church and, in the capital, Copenhagen, this drops to around 1 per cent in church each Sunday. Similarly in Finland where nearly 94 per cent claim to be Lutherans but regular attendance is only 5 per cent with less than 1 per cent taking communion. In Norway, where Christianity is taught in the public schools, boys and girls are prepared for confirmation by the school and then confirmed in church. Unfortunately, this is the last time many of them are seen in church.

In Germany, home of the Reformation, many parishes have 4,000 people claiming allegiance to the state church and yet only about 100 of these are in church each Sunday. The churches have some contact with a further 300 but this leaves 3,600 with no Christian contact at all. West Germany is a nation where a tax is levied by the state on all those who belong (or nominally belong) to the Church, i.e. those baptised as infants. About 1 per cent each year are opting not to pay this tax and are thus deleted from church membership.

It is difficult to obtain accurate figures for Eastern Europe but there is evidence of considerable growth among Pentecostals and Baptists, as well as an expansion of the renewal movement in the Catholic church. Despite persecution from the authorities, there is no doubt that there has been an overall growth in the number of committed Christians and in church attendance during the past twenty-five years.

Britain
In Britain, church attendance has been in decline for most of this century, particularly since 1940. Following the Second World War there was some recovery but by

the end of the 1950s the pattern of decline accelerated until it reached the all-time low of 11 per cent in 1979. Since then there has been no comprehensive survey covering all the denominations, but small-scale samples and denominational figures indicate some significant changes in the overall picture. The figures for the MARC Census of the English Churches taken in 1989 should be available at the beginning of the 1990s, and will probably confirm these changes.

On the one hand, the mainline denominations – the Church of England, the Methodist Church, the United Reformed Church, the Catholic Church, the Church of Wales and the Church of Scotland – have all continued to decline through the 1980s although there are indications that the rate of decline has slowed. This is mainly accounted for by the considerable growth among some evangelicals and those churches that have moved into charismatic renewal. The Baptist Church is the only mainline denomination in England that has shown a slight but steady growth since 1980. In Northern Ireland, however, all the churches show attendance that is higher than anywhere else in the UK, but this has to be seen in relation to the social and political situation in the Province.

On the other hand, among the newer churches there has been considerable growth. Included among these are the Pentecostals, the new Independent groups of fellowships that have grown out of the house churches, and the ethnic churches.

The past twenty-five years have seen considerable changes in the overall situation of the church in Britain. The changes have mainly been in a shift from the strength of the mainline churches to the growing strength of the newer churches and related organisations. For example, despite the closure of many churches by the mainline denominations, particularly in inner-city areas, many new fellowships have been planted, mainly by the newer churches, so the decline has been more than offset and today there are more churches in the UK than there were ten years ago. During this period many churches that began as house churches meeting in homes have now acquired their own buildings in order to accommodate their increased numbers.

In terms of personnel, although there has been a considerable decline in the number of ordained clergy in the mainstream churches, this has been more than offset by the vast increase in the number of full-time Christian workers in the newer churches and evangelistic organisations carrying out a wide range of mission activities. This situation is reflected in the decline in the numbers of ordinands attending theological colleges and the consequent closure of many of these institutions. But this has been offset by the very considerable increase in the number of students attending Bible colleges in the UK during the past twenty years, and the expansion in the number of Bible schools.

There has been a decline in the number of main-stream church-related bodies, such as overseas missionary societies and home mission organisations, but this has been counterbalanced by the growth of established organisations, such as the Bible Society, Scripture Union and the Evangelical Alliance, alongside the birth of numerous newer para-church organisations, such as Youth With a Mission, British Youth For Christ, Operation Mobilisation, and many others working alongside the churches and providing valuable resources.

In the hard-pressed inner-city areas of Britain, which have been experiencing a wide range of social problems, there has been a high rate of closure of churches belonging to the mainstream denominations although this has slowed down since 1980. In many of these areas, church attendance in the 1970s dropped to a mere half of 1 per cent due, in part, to the movement of Christians out to the suburbs and the inflow of immigrants of other faiths from the Commonwealth.

There are indications today of growth among Pentecostal and Charismatic fellowships but the most
notable growth has been in the ethnic churches under
Afro-Caribbean leadership.

Despite all the evidence of growth and fresh vitality
in many sectors of the church's life and work in
Britain, the number of regular church-goers today is
still not as great as it was ten years ago, and is
considerably less than it was at the beginning of the
twentieth century. The movement to nominality and
then out of the Church, which took place earlier this
century, will not be reversed easily and it could take a
long time to recover the position the Church previously
occupied in the life of the nation.

Loss of Significance
A realistic assessment of the state of the Church in
Britain cannot be gained without taking into account
the overall loss of social significance during the
second half of this century. Until 1950, the Church
occupied a position of incalculable significance in
every sphere of life. All the major social institutions in
Britain were based upon Christian principles and
influenced largely by the Church.

The British legal system and concepts of justice and
social morality were all founded upon the teachings of
Christianity. These concepts have been eroded both by
the onslaught of secularism and by the loss of the
social influence of the Church, which is reflected in
the basic changes in family life, marriage breakdown,
child abuse, abortion and lower standards of personal
and public morality as well as by many changes in the
law revoking some of those with a Christian basis.

The first schools were established by the churches.
Even though most of these were taken over by the State
in the first half of this century, they still reflected
biblical principles until changes in legislation in the
second half of this century began to reflect secular

humanist values. The 1944 Education Act insisted that every child should be given instruction in biblical Christianity and should participate in a daily act of Christian worship unless specifically withdrawn by their parents. There have been problems in enforcing this Act so that this now happens in very few schools and is a reflection of both the multi-faith character of modern Britain and the secular forces which have become predominant today. In reaction to this, and in an attempt to re-establish Christian standards, a number of churches have opened schools as a Christian alternative, but these are usually quite small in numbers and limited in resources.

During the first half of this century, the Church was influential in every sphere of public life not simply in matters of belief and morality but also in matters of social concern such as welfare, human rights, social reform and in matters of political debate. Clergy and ministers served on many public committees and played an important part in local community affairs as well as in the life of the nation. Even as late as 1962 this was still happening as, for example, in the appointment of the Archbishop of Canterbury as Chairman of the National Committee for Commonwealth Immigrants, as noted in Chapter Two. Today, fewer and fewer Christian leaders are expected to lead in the affairs of the State or to take positions in public office. The contribution it is felt they can make to the life of the nation is minimal and compartmentalised.

In fact, the practice of Christianity in Britain has become very much a fringe occupation in the private domain. Its public influence has become marginalised on a par with the 'God slot' among TV programmes. Real life is secular and Christianity is increasingly seen as a hobby on a par with 'DIY' or the golf club, and reserved for a limited period of time in a particular place.

The British experience of the decline in social influence of the Church during this century is paralleled throughout the nations of Europe. The forces of secularisation have removed the Church from a position of power and authority; social and moral values that were based upon the Gospel have been replaced by secular values. In 1985, a Norwegian pastor was prosecuted for declaring homosexuality to be sinful. He was found guilty of breaking the law and given a suspended prison sentence and warned not to speak of such things in public again.

In Holland, Amsterdam is known as the pornographic and prostitution centre of Europe. Travel agents actually use the 'red light district' as a major tourist attraction in their brochures and yet Amsterdam was a major European centre of Reformation Faith. It was the home of the Pilgrim Fathers shortly before their historic journey from Plymouth to America in the *Mayflower* in AD 1620.

At the beginning of the century, the nations of Europe were renowned throughout the world as the most devout adherents of the Christian faith; today Europe is the most secular continent in the world. There can be few examples in the whole of history of more radical change in so short a period, as the way in which Europe has abandoned its Christian heritage and the biblical principles upon which the nations were founded.

Historical Perspectives

The history of the Christian Church is not one of *steady* growth from a handful of disciples on the day of Pentecost, to one third of the world's population today. Rather it has been a record of growth and decline like the ebb and flow of the tide, with each fresh wave reaching a new high-water mark.

The seven volumes of Kenneth Latourette's *History*

of the Expansion of Christianity make fascinating reading showing the advances and recessions of the Christian faith down through the ages.

Period of Decline

The periods of decline after a great surge forward are often linked with the decline of an empire or major political power with which Christianity had become closely linked, and which had also been seen as the promoter or protector of the Christian faith.

The Church grew rapidly during the first five centuries and then suffered a recession with the defeat of the Roman Empire. The Greek Orthodox church, which was very strong until the thirteenth century, declined with the Byzantine Empire, the fall of which helped the Muslim advance of that period. The decline of Spain and Portugal heralded the third major recession in the mid-1700s. The declining influence of northern Europe on the world scene in the 1900s, and, in particular, the demise of the British Empire and the loss of European colonies, has been accompanied by a decline in the western Church.

One lesson to be learned from this, and which the western missionaries have had to learn, is that in order for a church to survive changes of government it must be indigenised and become a part of the local culture.

In the eighteenth and nineteenth centuries, which were the eras of the greatest expansion of the missionary movement from Europe, the conversion of the heathen and the social betterment of the underprivileged went hand-in-hand. It was not until this century that any dichotomy was seen between them.

Western imperialism often accompanied the Gospel, and oppressed the people in countries where the missionaries were working. This had the effect of aligning the church with western colonialism in the minds of the people so that when independence came, the Church suffered the same fate as the defeated occupying force. This was the experience in India where the church today is only slowly becoming indigenised more than forty years after independence.

Wherever the Church becomes closely allied to a secular power its fate is bound up with that of the political rulers. This is what happened in Ethiopia when the government of Emperor Haile Selassie was overthrown by a communist coup. Christians were persecuted because the Church was seen to be an opposing force loyal to the Emperor.

The Church has to maintain a distance from worldly authorities because the spiritual and the worldly cannot be married. Jesus said, 'My Kingdom is not of this world' (John 18:36). Where men try to identify the Kingdom with the world, it leads to disaster.

Periods of Advance

Latourette traces four great periods of advance in the history of the expansion of Christianity until the early part of the twentieth century. The Initial Advance, covering the first five centuries, began at Pentecost with the outpouring of the Holy Spirit upon all believers. In was the impetus of the Holy Spirit and the conviction of the first disciples that they were witnesses to the resurrection of Jesus, combined with the effects of persecution, that carried the Gospel from Judea throughout the Roman world until the political structure of the Empire began to crumble.

The Second Great Age of Advance from AD 950 to AD 1350, Latourette attributes to a reforming zeal that stemmed from a revival that began in the monastery at Cluny. The revival soon spread beyond the monasteries and permeated through the Church. It not only brought about stricter monastic life, but cleansed the Church of many corrupt and worldly influences which in turn spilled over into fresh evangelistic outreach.

The Third Great Age of Advance from AD 1500 to AD 1750 is attributable to the Reformation with its attempt to reproduce the purity of New Testament Christianity. The Reformation was essentially a biblical movement and coincided with a fresh study of the Greek manuscripts of the New Testament. The Reformers' emphasis upon faith in Jesus as the only basis of salvation gave a fresh impetus to save the lost, and a new wave of reforming zeal that swept through the church. Most Protestants think of the Reformation as the time of the birth of the Protestant churches, whereas Catholics regard it as the period of the 'great schism', but there is evidence that much of the renewed spiritual life remained within the Roman Catholic church and it was a period of general spiritual growth that generated more than two centuries of advance.

The Fourth Great Age of Advance from AD 1815 to AD 1914 was the age of the European missionary movement when the Gospel was carried to all the areas of European colonisation. The missionary movement not only planted churches but also founded schools and hospitals, caring for the educational and physical needs of the people as part of the outworking of the Gospel. It was an age of great confidence when European Christians believed that God had commissioned them to carry the light of the Gospel to the darkest parts of the world.

Latourette's study was completed before the middle of the twentieth century but today we are able to discern the Fifth Great Age of Advance that began about 1960. It coincided with the movement for independence among nations that were former European colonies, and the struggle for freedom among the oppressed. It also coincided with a rediscovery of the power of the Holy Spirit, which began with the Pentecostal movement in the 1920s an spilled over into the Charismatic renewal movement in the 1960s, that has had a great influence upon most branches of the Church, and has been responsible for the planting of many new churches. The present advance may, in the future, be known as the new age of the Holy Spirit.

The two major points that come through are that each age of advance is characterised by a fresh spiritual experience which generates a renewed confidence in the Gospel, and an urge to communicate the faith resulting in both reforming established practices and a new movement of outreach.

Biblical Witness

Jesus left his disciples with both a command and a strategy for world evangelisation.

The Command

'All authority in heaven and on earth has been given to me. Therefore go and make disciples of all nations, baptising them in the name of the Father and of the Son and of the Holy Spirit, and teaching them to obey everything I have commanded you. And surely I am with you always, until the very end of the age' (Matt. 28:18-20).

The Strategy

'But you will receive power when the Holy Spirit comes on you; and you will be my witnesses in Jersualem, and in all Judea and Samaria, and to the ends of the earth' (Acts 1:8).

Jesus' command to the disciples contained in the Great Commission provided the Church with its 'raison d'être'. The disciples knew themselves to be witnesses to the resurrection of Jesus, to the forgiveness of sin and to the new life that was available to all believers through him. Jesus' command was to communicate this good news to people of all nations. Thus the disciples saw themselves as the Ambassadors of the Kingdom.

The Power

But the disciples not only received the command to go. Jesus also gave them the strategy for the mission and the power to accomplish it. In his last instruction to them before the Ascension, he told them to wait in Jerusalem until the Father fulfilled his promise to send the power of the Holy Spirit upon them which would enable them to be his witnesses in a world hostile to the Gospel. The strategy for growth was to begin where they were, preaching the good news in the city where Jesus had proclaimed the Kingdom, witnessed to its leaders, cleansed the temple and been crucified and had risen from the dead.

They were then to move out by stages: first to their neighbours in the province of Judea with whom they shared a common language, beliefs and traditions; then to Samaria where although the language was identical, tradition and culture were different. The final stage of the strategy was to carry the Gospel to foreign nations where they would be breaking all the barriers of language, culture and religion.

Jesus knew that the only way in which the Great Commission could be fulfilled was in the power of the Holy Spirit. Hence his warning not to go in their own strength but to wait for the Spirit to come upon them at Pentecost.

The Early Church

The record of the expansion of the Church given in the Acts of the Apostles shows how the disciples actually followed the strategy given by Jesus. The Gospel went from Jerusalem throughout Judea and Samaria, then to Antioch which became the springboard for the missions of Paul, Barnabas, Silas and others into the Gentile world. The early Church not only expanded across the globe but it also grew in numbers. As the Church grew stronger both in faith and in numbers, it was being prepared for more work.

Growth is the work of God, not man. The Church, the body, grows as God causes it to grow (Col. 2:19). Jesus taught that the lilies of the field grew because God took care of them. Paul refers to the controversy among the leaders in Corinth as to who was responsible for finding all the new converts, and he reminds them that they could sow the seed, they could also water it, but only God could make it grow (1 Cor. 3:6).

Numerical growth is often the most spectacular, but growth in numbers is not enough; Christians need to grow in the grace and knowledge of their Lord and Saviour Jesus Christ (2 Peter 3:18 and Col. 1:10). They also need to grow in faith (2 Thess. 1:3). When the body is fully dependent upon Christ it will grow and be built up in love as each part does its work (Eph. 4:16).

Underlying Principles

There are numerous lessons that can be learned from studying the patterns of growth. Those involved in the church-growth movement are always keenly interested in discovering new truths which can help remove some of the barriers which we erect and which prevent God growing his church.

Three of the outstanding underlying principles of growth that emerge from the examples given in the preceding sections are *expectation, obedience and humility*.

A major growth factor is that of *expectation*. If we do not expect to grow, then we will not be disappointed when we don't. But if we expect great things of God, he will not disappoint us. In Europe, where the churches have been immersed in rational intellectualism, there is a low expectation of God. He is not seen as being in control of the nations or even of the Church. God is not expected to be able to answer prayer or even to build his Church. This contrasts strongly with the expectations of Christians in those parts of the world where spiritual awakening is taking place.

Another underlying principle is *obedience*. The Great Commission lays emphasis upon this. Jesus followed his command to 'make disciples' with the instruction to 'teach them to obey'. We are not just to teach all that God has taught us, but we are also to teach people to *obey* God's word. Understanding and wanting to follow Christ results in obedience to all that he wants us to be and to do. We cannot love God and not obey him, as John 14:21 makes clear.

Another principle which seems to be especially appropriate for Christians in the western nations is *humility*. Western Christians need to develop a willingness to learn from those who are younger in the faith, but who are full of the power of the Holy Spirit. Europeans are no longer the world's teachers, but need to become students once again and, in humility, learn from those whom they once taught. The Galatians needed to learn this, 'Anyone who receives instruction in the word must share all good things with his instructor' (6:6). Even the most mature Christian, or the most learned theologian, can learn from the newest believer. But it requires a depth of spiritual humility to be able to receive. Many Christians find it easier to give, and very hard to receive.

Questions

1 In what ways has the growth and decline of the Church in many nations, and in your own in particular, been affected by social changes since the end of World War Two?

2 A number of new models of the Church have developed in recent years (e.g. the megachurches and prayer mountains of South Korea) using different

concepts and methods. In what ways, if any, has the church in your own nation been affected by these?

3 God grows his church. What are the human barriers to the work of God?

4 Discuss the different aspects of growth in the Church and the various signs of growth today.

5 The Church thrives when it becomes indigenous. Missionaries have learned the fallacy of taking their own culture along with the Gospel when working overseas. What lessons are there in this for Christians in this country?

6 In the European nations there are large numbers of nominal Christians and the churches have become marginalised. How do you account for this? How can nominal Christians be reactivated and dormant churches revitalised?

7 On the day of Pentecost, 3,000 were added to the Church (Acts 2:41). Is numerical growth always good and is it the most significant pointer to spiritual vitality?

8 In this chapter the basic principles underlying growth were noted as 'expectation', 'obedience' and 'humility'. Can you discern others?

Chapter Five

Spiritual Power

*My message and my preaching were not with wise
and persuasive words, but with a demonstration of
the Spirit's power, so that your faith might not rest
on men's wisdom, but on God's power.*

I Cor. 2:4-5

Rich Christians

One of the major characteristics apparent in Christian
fellowships in the 'two-thirds-world', which appears
to be largely absent in the West, is the power of the
Holy Spirit and the evidence of signs and wonders.

In the early days of the renewal movement, currently
sweeping through most churches in Singapore, I
discussed the situation with Bishop Chiu Ban It, the
former Bishop of Singapore. He described how the
first evidence of the Holy Spirit had been seen among
high school children and how, in 1972, his own
spiritual life had been transformed. The whole life of
the Cathedral was affected and soon began to spread
through the diocese. I asked him if they were seeing
signs and wonders in the Anglican churches. He
paused, and then said, 'It would be a wonder if there
were no signs!'

When the Spirit of God is moving in power across a
nation, signs and wonders are part of the everyday
experience of Christians. They are not seen as abnormal,
but as normal. Believers expect to see the evidence of
the power of God at work in their own lives and in the

life of the Christian community. It is this natural expectation that underlies their faith.

Power in China
Pastor Samuel Lam, whose faith under persecution was referred to in Chapter Two, has many stories to tell of the power of God at work in China today. His house-church congregation has grown rapidly since 1980, and the whole work has been founded on faith and the confident expectation that the power of God that preserved him through the years of persecution is sufficient for all his needs.

He told me how one day he was asked to visit an elderly woman who had been bedridden for ten years. She was not a Christian, so he began by telling her about the Lord Jesus and shared his own testimony of faith in God. She accepted Jesus as her Saviour and then he began to pray for her. Whilst he was praying he felt God saying that he was to take her by the hand and tell her to stand up and walk. He did this and the power of God entered her and strength returned to her legs. The following Sunday, she walked to his church, an hour's walk away, and was baptised. The whole congregation knew that this was a notable miracle as the woman was eighty years of age.

Pastor Lam told me of many other instances of the power of God in the lives of believers, both young and old. He spoke of two young girls who had been working in the fields through the day, and were returning home towards evening when they were attacked by three men who were bent on raping them. They were both believers and in great fear they cried out to the Lord. Suddenly the three men were struck down.

The two girls ran back to their village and told the elders of their church what had happened. The elders asked the girls where the men were, and two of them went out and found the men lying in the field just as the girls had said. They prayed over them, and the men, looking bewildered sat up. The elders told them that they had been struck down by the power of God because of their wickedness, and that only Jesus could forgive sin. The men listened quietly while the elders told them the Gospel, and each of them was led to Christ. Their conversion made an impact on the whole village because these three men were notorious for their bad behaviour. Their conversion led to many others in the village receiving Christ.

The Christian community throughout China today, abounds with stories about the power of God being released through the faith of believers – sometimes in the most amazing ways. On one occasion, the family of a woman who was very ill sent for a pastor from a neighbouring town. By the time he received the message and reached the village the woman was already dead. Her body had been laid outside the house as was the custom in that part of China. Four communist officials were interrogating members of the family and taking details of the woman's death. She was known to be a Christian, and the officials took the opportunity of heaping abuse upon the woman's sons.

When the pastor eventually arrived he, too, became the butt of their jibes. They knew a little about the Christian faith and particularly that Jesus was reputed to have risen from the dead. They thought they would have a little more fun at the expense of these simple Christians. They challenged the pastor, 'If your God is so great that he can raise people from the dead, why don't you pray for her and raise her too?'

The pastor was a simple, Bible-believing man, who had never been to theological college. Without another word he began to pray over the woman's body. Suddenly she sat up. The communist officials were terrified and ran screaming up the road. She said that she had been to the gates of heaven, and wanted to tell them all about it, but first she would prepare a meal for them all. After the family's meal of thanksgiving, the woman gave her testimony, not just to her family but to the whole village who had gathered by that time. The pastor took the opportunity of preaching the Gospel – 'the power of God for the salvation of everyone who believes' (Romans 1:16) – which led to the conversion of practically everyone in the village including three of the four communist officials.

Power in Nigeria
The power of God does not depend upon the laying on of hands or even upon the intercession of believers. There are many examples of the power of God coming down upon the people in large meetings. Evangelist Benson Idahosa has seen this happen many times in large crusade meetings that he has led in different parts of Nigeria. Reference has already been made in Chapter Four to the large numbers attending crusade meetings in Nigeria, sometimes as many as half a million people at a single meeting resulting in thousands giving their lives to Christ each night. This turning to God has also been accompanied by many demonstrations of God's healing power. In such large meetings it is not possible for the sick to be prayed for individually. This is how a secular reporter in the Nigerian *Evening Sketch* described one night in the Olabadun Stadium in Ibadan.

'Archbishop Idahosa had not even started to pray when the power of the Almighty descended on the overcrowded stadium. He was still speaking from the Gospel of Luke, about Jesus catching the anger of the scribes and Pharisees, when a thunderous 'Hallelujah' tore the air from a section of the stadium. Archbishop Idahosa quickly said, "A miracle has happened there". And that is how avalanches of wonders started rolling through the night, left, centre and everywhere in the stadium. There were wonders unlimited, miracles unimaginable.

'I saw vividly two women regain their sight; four

93

paralysed boys walked; two deaf mutes heard and began speaking; a teenage girl struck down by paralysis over nine years ago walked. There were hundreds of other miracles but because of the packed crowds, those healed could not mount the rostrum to give their testimony.

'One woman, who regained her sight, said she had been blind for more than ten years. When asked to give her name to the *Evening Sketch*, she shouted "Name! My name! What does that matter! I can see you now! You are holding a camera. You are wearing a shirt." And that was how it went on far into the night as the power of God came down upon the whole company.'

Power in Indonesia

The power of God is not only to be seen in healings but also in other miraculous events. When the expectation of believers is unlimited so too is the power of God that is available to his people. Dr Petrus Octavianus describes how he discovered that the power of God can be released through faith. He was one of the pioneer evangelists in the early days of the revival in Indonesia.

He travelled from city to city and from island to island preaching the Gospel wherever he could draw a crowd. He recalls how he stayed one night in a woodland retreat during a series of meetings which he was finding particularly exhausting. It was a beautiful, quiet place in peaceful countryside, and he expected to be able to regain his strength through a good night's rest. But as darkness fell all the frogs in the neighbourhood seemed to awake. The noise of their croaking filled the night sky. Sleep was impossible and he began to pray earnestly for God to make them quiet. But the noise continued. His prayers went unanswered and he began to cry out to God for understanding. At that point, he felt God saying to him, '*Command* them to stop in my Name'. For some time he resisted but sleep was impossible, so, finally, feeling rather foolish, he went outside and pointing his finger at the swamp, he said in a loud voice, which could be heard all over the compound, 'Frogs, in the Name of Jesus I command you to be quiet'. Suddenly there was silence, much to the amazement of his companions who, on hearing his voice, had come outside to see what was happening. Silence reigned for the rest of the night!

Many of the meetings addressed by Petrus Octavianus were held in the open air where there was no protection from those who wanted to disrupt the meetings. Many of the Muslim population were hostile to the Gospel, and often attempted to break up evangelistic meetings. On one occasion there was a large group of infiltrators making a great deal of noise during the worship, and he wondered what would happen when he began to bring the message. He remembered how God had sealed the mouths of the frogs and he prayed that God would silence these men. Just before he began to speak he commanded them in the Name of the Lord Jesus to be quiet. God was faithful – the troublemakers were silenced – it was as though they were struck dumb, unable to move, or to utter any sound. They stood quietly throughout the preaching of the Gospel, and a number of them actually responded to the Word and committed their lives to the Lord Jesus.

Petrus said that his experience with the frogs taught him the power of God over the whole of nature, and this gave him the confidence to respond in faith each time he was faced with a difficult situation during his ministry as an evangelist.

On one occasion, an open-air stadium was packed with people, who had come to hear the Gospel, when torrential rain started to fall over the city. As heavy drops began descending on the stadium, the crowd started to scatter and it was obvious that the meeting would have to be abandoned if the rain continued. The platform party prayed for the rain to stop – and once again Petrus believed God was telling him to issue a command. He pointed to the clouds and commanded them in the Name of the Lord Jesus to disperse. The whole crowd in the stadium heard him make this declaration of faith and to their utter amazement a gap appeared in the dark clouds and although it continued to rain in the area all round, the stadium remained dry. Needless to say, multitudes became believers that night!

The idea that the power of God can be exercised over the weather is anathema to the minds of many western Christians. The western mind is closed to the possibility of God intervening to redirect the forces that control the natural order of creation. Even those Christians who believe that God *could* do such a thing usually believe that he *would not*. Christians in countries, such as Indonesia, where the power of God is everywhere to be seen, are not troubled with philosophical arguments. They simply believe.

A Norwegian missionary who has spent twelve years in Indonesia, a man of considerable academic achievement, confessed to me that when he goes back to Norway he dare not speak about some of the things he has witnessed in Indonesia for fear that he will be laughed to scorn. He says that he has seen the most amazing evidence of the power of God over evil spirits. At evangelistic meetings when people are converted from the pagan animistic religions, the most incredible things sometimes happen that if he had not witnessed with his own eyes he would find impossible to believe.

Many of the local religions involve demonic practices. Often needles are inserted below the skin to ward off evil spirits, and children are made to swallow fetishes which lodge in their stomachs and procure, for the children, the favour of a particular god. He has seen the Spirit of God come upon newly converted believers with such power that these charms have been involuntarily vomited out of their bodies, and he has also seen needles popping out of their skin and falling on the floor. This has happened without any effort on the part of the new believer. He believes that it is direct evidence of the power of the Holy Spirit over the forces of darkness, cleansing the new believer from the spiritual forces that used to hold him in bondage.

Poor Christians

The Norwegian pastor quoted above said that he would now find it very difficult to minister to a church in Norway, and he hopes to stay in South East Asia where the power of God is at work. He said that Europeans, especially the men with whom he trained in theological college, would think him crazy if he tried to describe such happenings. 'Europeans', he said, 'simply do not believe in the power of the Holy Spirit'.

The sophisticated western mind seeks a rational explanation for everything. Miraculous events are explained away or dismissed as unbelievable. The westerner can only believe things for which there is sound scientific evidence.

My son was a pupil at Dean Close School, Cheltenham, when a boy broke his thumb in a rugby match. He was taken to Cheltenham General Hospital where his head was x-rayed, and the broken bone was set and put in plaster. A few days later he attended a meeting in Bath where my husband was speaking. He went forward for ministry and was so convinced he had been healed he stripped off the plaster and began using the thumb normally.

On returning to school, he reported to the matron who was so anxious not to be blamed if anything went wrong, that she took him back to the hospital to see the doctor, and told him what had happened. The thumb was x-rayed and there was no sign of a break. The doctor refused to believe it had been healed and said he must have been mistaken when he had put it in plaster the previous week. When the matron asked him to check the original x-ray he said it has been lost.

The Headmaster of Dean Close School said that it appeared that the hospital authorities preferred to admit to medical incompetence and an administrative blunder, rather than accept that a miracle of healing had taken place. This illustrates the extent to which secularisation has penetrated the thinking of Europeans who find it impossible to accept any evidence of the supernatural that is linked with faith in God.

There is, however, considerable interest in what may be broadly described as the 'paranormal'. Horoscopes are immensely popular, not only in Britain, but throughout the West. Millions of sophisticated westerners opening their morning newspaper, turn first to see what the stars forecast for their day. There are very few westerners who are thorough-going atheists; most people accept some kind of belief in the supernatural, even if it is little more than superstition. They have a vague awareness of spiritual forces outside the control of rational thought. Only a small minority of westerners would claim to be totally 'liberated' from what Marx regarded as the 'bondage' of religion. Most westerners live in a world of secular materialism that wholly occupies their thinking, their values and ambitions, yet at the 'breaking points' of life – birth, marriage and death – they usually turn to religion for nurture and comfort.

Factual Analyses
Social surveys indicate that very few Europeans have finally rejected religion even though they no longer follow the beliefs and practices of their forbears. Church attendance throughout Europe is very low today compared with a century ago, but few people admit to having no belief in God.

Gallup UK carried out a *European Value Systems*

Study in 1981 which showed that 76 per cent of British people believed in God. A further, more limited, study for Marplan on *Religious Beliefs in Britain* in November 1986 found very similar results in that almost 80 per cent said they believed in God, 70 per cent acknowledged a belief in 'sin', and more than half declared that they believed in miracles.

The figures quoted above relate to the general population but, even among regular churchgoers, the inroads of secularisation undermining faith in God are apparent. This is particularly so among the clergy and those who have undergone a theological education. Studies in America have shown higher levels of belief among the laity than the clergy. A survey of representatives attending a conference of the National Council of Churches in the United States showed that 78 per cent of the laity had no doubts at all about a belief in God, as compared with 62 per cent of clergy in pastoral charge; but only 33 per cent of laity said they believed in miracles while a mere 24 per cent of pastoral clergy shared this belief. The survey showed that ordained ministers holding administrative positions had even less belief than those in pastoral charge. (*The Gathering Storm in the Church*, Jeffrey Hadden pp.228-230 Doubleday, New York 1970)

It is interesting to note that those clergy who were in administrative positions within the church had more doubts on fundamental tenets of faith than the pastoral clergy, yet these are the men who hold real power in the church, particularly in terms of policy making. They control selection procedures for ordinands as well as the appointment of office bearers and training programmes for the clergy.

The storm that Jeffrey Hadden foresaw gathering in the churches back in 1970 was rooted in the unbelief of the clergy whose doubts were being communicated to the laity and thus were spreading like a cancer through the Church, and out into the general population. This has happened throughout western society, and is particularly evident in Europe where theological scepticism began in the latter part of the eighteenth century and developed throughout the nineteenth century giving birth to the Form Criticism School of German theologians, such as Baultmann and his successors.

Intellecturalism

Tens of thousands of clergy have been trained in theological colleges throughout Europe and America by academic theologians, who do not regard the Bible as the authentic word of God, and who do not have a strong personal experience of faith in God. This has resulted in a lack of biblical preaching and teaching in the mainline churches. The clergy have also been active in voicing their doubts on some of the foundational Christian beliefs and this has undermined the faith of millions of western Christians. In the American survey mentioned above, nearly half of the ordained ministers in administrative positions did not believe in the 'divinity of Jesus' or even in 'life after death'. Liberal intellectualism has spread far beyond the church into the general population of the western nations. It is perhaps one of the strangest paradoxes of all time that the veracity of biblical Christianity has been attacked from *within* the church rather than from outside. Unbelief has spread into the secular world largely from those who profess to be believers and who bear the responsibility for teaching the faith to others.

If the preachers do not believe the word of God and have no concept of a personal God who is present and active in the world today and whose power is available to all believers, they will not be effective in communicating a living faith. This does not mean that all biblical scholarship undermines faith, but rather that the pursuit of theological knowledge as a mere intellectual exercise outside the context of a living faith in God, leads to the kind of sterile intellectualism that characterises large sectors of the church today.

Belief in Power

There is, however, one major sector of the church which not only believes the Bible to be the authentic word of God but also believes in the power of God through the Holy Spirit being presently available to all believers. This is the Pentecostal and Charismatic sector which has been growing rapidly worldwide since the middle of this century. In the Charismatic and Pentecostal churches there is plenty of evidence of the power of God to be seen. It is comparatively easy to find Christians who have been healed of cancer, of blindness, of deafness, or who were lame and now walk normally, or who have been healed of a variety of physical ailments or abnormal states of mind.

Accounts of such things rarely find their way into the media despite the secular interest in the paranormal. The reason for the failure of the press to give publicity to these miracles is because Christians always give account of them in the context of personal faith and give the glory to God. The secular press is happy to publish accounts of those who have overcome physical disability through their own strength or through acts of will power but they are not interested in the testimony of Christians who emphasise their dependence upon God. The secular media prefers to ridicule God rather than acknowledge his existence and power.

The gathering storm of the 1960s and 1970s broke in the church during the 1980s but there is, nevertheless, evidence today that the movement of the Holy Spirit, that is sweeping through many nations in the non-western world, is also beginning to have an impact upon the western nations. Today, there is increasing recognition being given to the theory of 'waves' of spiritual revival. Within the major waves distinguished by Latourette (noted in Chapter Four) there are a number of smaller subsidiary waves. The incoming tide moves forward in a series of waves of different dimensions each reaching new high-water marks. A similar thing is happening today in the overall growth of the Church and the expansion of spiritual life and faith within the Church.

Three particular waves of spiritual activity can be discerned in the twentieth century. The First Wave brought a fresh anointing of the Spirit with the Pentecostal movement of the 1920s, and the recognition of spiritual gifts.

The Second Wave started in the 1960s with the rise of the Charismatic movement that emphasised the availability to all believers of the gifts of the Holy Spirit. This second wave, although confined to the Body of Christ, left no sector of the church untouched.

The Third Wave, which began in the 1980s, is having an even wider influence. On the one hand, it is touching many churches not caught up in the first two waves, revitalising their worship, witness and fellowship life. As evidence of this it is noteworthy that by 1988 more than half of all the Anglican ordinands training for the ministry in Britain were evangelicals, most of whom were also charismatic. On the other hand, it is widening the vision of members in the renewed churches and giving a greater urgency to evangelism, a fresh emphasis on mission and a desire for community service.

The Future for the West
It may be that the way is being prepared for revival that will affect whole nations. This is the hope and fervent prayer of multitudes of Christians throughout Europe and America, who hear of what God is doing in other parts of the world, who know their own rich spiritual heritage, and who long for God to move in power once again in the western nations.

Nevertheless the strength of the barriers to spiritual

revival in the western nations of America and Europe, including Britain, needs to be recognised. The intellectual heritage stemming from the eighteenth century Enlightenment that produced rationalist systems of thought that have dominated the West, has left what appears to be an indelible mark. It has not only produced the secular humanism that characterises much of western thinking today, but it has had a singular influence upon all sections of the Christian church. Reference has already been made to the strong influence of biblical criticism upon theology, the extreme form of which was the 'God is Dead' movement of the 1960s. The demythologising of the Gospel resulted in the depersonalising of God so that God was seen as an impersonal force. He was 'the wholly other' separated from the ordinary spheres of human activity. He was the mystery underlying the universe and the whole of creation, and as such he was unknowable to ordinary mortal human beings. Thus the desire to know God and to be in close communion with him became an intellectual exercise, a striving for the mastery of philosophical systems to know the great unknowable.

Although evangelicals would strenuously deny any contamination from what they see as the errors of liberal theology, the influence of secular rationalism in theological systems has undoubtedly had its effect upon what may be broadly termed the 'bible-believing' sector of the church. Evangelical scholars have striven to match the thinking of liberal theologians by defending the biblical basis of faith on intellectual grounds. They have thereby tacitly admitted that intellect and rational argument are the final criteria of truth. Thus even among evangelicals, a form of biblical intellectualism has replaced the simple basis of faith in Jesus as Lord and Saviour and the life-changing experience of the presence and power of Christ. Thus 'head-knowledge' has become more important than the experience of the power of God in the life of the believer.

Many evangelicals not only mistrust, but actually have a fear of, the experiential. This largely accounts for the rabid anti-charismatic attitude found among many evangelical intellectuals. The great danger of this is that is can lead to a kind of 'pharisaic legalism' with rigid attitudes towards biblical doctrine that leave no room for the Holy Spirit to bring fresh enlightenment. In attempting to guard the church against the excesses of the purely experiential, many evangelicals have retreated into the opposite error of biblical rationalism. Jesus spoke sternly to the biblical intellectuals of his day – 'Woe to you experts in the law, because you have taken away the key to knowledge. You yourselves have not entered, and you have hindered those who were entering' (Luke 11:52). To know the word of God while denying the presence and power of God in the life of the believer is to rob the word of God of power. As Paul reminded the Corinthians, true faith does 'not rest on men's wisdom but on God's power' (1 Cor. 2:5).

Christians who are not fully alive to the presence of the Holy Spirit in the church today and his activity, are rather like a household that is experiencing a power cut. All the right equipment is there, sufficient for light to illuminate the house and far beyond, but no power is being received to make it happen.

Historical Perspectives

Historically, the power of God has been available to all believers since the day of Pentecost. This was the witness of Peter to the crowd in Jerusalem. The record of events in the Acts of the Apostles bears testimony to the reality of spiritual power in the early church. The signs and wonders that were the manifestation of God's power were the every-day experience of believers

104

in the New Testament churches. The power of God accompanied a strong sense of the presence of the Lord among the believers. They were witnesses to all the Lord had said and done. He was alive and lived amongst them. His power was to be seen in their lives. It was the Lord Jesus who spoke through them and it was his power that was released as they prayed and laid hands on the sick, and witnessed before the people and the governing authorities. It was the power of God among his people that brought glory to the Name of Jesus.

A major characteristic of the New Testament church was that of spiritual power being exercised by the whole community of believers. By the end of the first century and the close of the writing of the New Testament, the life of the Christian community was beginning to be regulated by the development of fixed forms of worship, and by the establishment of full-time leaders, who were seen as the guardians and defenders of the faith.

Over the next two centuries, the position and power of leaders became firmly established and, at the same time, the exercise of spiritual gifts by all believers faded. By the end of the third century, the practice of spiritual gifts was confined to small minority groups such as the Montanists, and spiritual power was only exercised by the ordained clergy. The power of God was to be seen in the lives of individuals rather than in the life of the Christian community as a whole. The lives of the saints and the great reformers bear testimony to this but throughout the centuries whenever there has been a revival, spiritual power has become not simply a possession of a few individuals, but also of the multitude of believers. This, in fact, has become a characteristic of revivals – that the Holy Spirit is poured out on all believers; the power of God comes down upon the whole community.

Revivals sometimes begin with the experience of spiritual power in the life of a single individual or a small group of believers which spills over to affect others and then becomes a general outpouring.

This is how the Wesleyan Revival began in eighteenth-century Britain. It was the power of God that brought a dramatic change into John Wesley's life on the occasion when he felt his heart 'strangely warmed' at the Moravian meeting in Aldersgate. From then on his ministry was transformed as God took control of his life. The contagion of the Holy Spirit spread rapidly and large crowds gathered wherever Wesley or his companions preached. There are many accounts of the power of God coming down upon whole companies of believers through the ministry of Wesley and his contemporary revivalist, Whitefield.

The Revival in Wales at the beginning of the twentieth century had the same effect on thousands of miners in the Welsh valleys. The hearts of hard-bitten men were melted by the power of God entering their lives. Whole communities were transformed as the Spirit of God came upon them.

The Welsh Revival was short-lived and never really penetrated far into England. It was running against the strong tide of advancing secularism and humanistic intellectualism that has characterised most of this century.

Two world wars and the development of weapons of horrific mass destruction sapped the self-confidence of mankind. The situation has been exacerbated by increasing economic difficulties, social problems, and violence in society that has created mounting disillusionment with humanism and man's ability to solve all problems. It is only in the closing decades of this century that the way has been opened for a revival of faith and for a fresh outpouring of the Holy Spirit and the power of God upon the whole body of believers.

Biblical Witness

In Chapter Four it was noted that the Great Commission provided the keynote for evangelism, not only for the believers in the New Testament church, but also for the spread of the Gospel throughout the centuries. Jesus not only gave the command to evangelise, he also gave the power to do it. In order to understand this, it is essential to note carefully the words at the beginning of the Acts of the Apostles where Jesus gave final instructions to his disciples (Acts 1:4). He told them to *wait* in Jerusalem until the Holy Spirit came upon them. The Holy Spirit would bring the power that would enable them to carry out the task which he had set them.

The experience of Pentecost brought radical changes to the lives of the disciples. There was no more hesitation. The waiting was over. God had fulfilled his promise. The power had come. The lives of all those who received the Holy Spirit were transformed. This can be seen most clearly in Peter. The impetuous, big fisherman became the leading spokesman of the church. The man with no learning gained great wisdom. The disciple who had denied Jesus in the High Priest's courtyard became the apostle who boldly faced the Sanhedrin and witnessed to the saving power of Messiah Jesus.

Peter's faith had sometimes risen to the heights, as when he stepped out of the boat and walked on the water at Jesus' invitation, and also when he was the first to acknowledge Jesus as the Messiah, but he was also the one whom Jesus called 'Satan' when he tried to dissuade Jesus from going to the cross – a name which Jesus had never even called the Pharisees! It was the experience of Pentecost that changed Peter into a strong, courageous leader in the early church. He did not stumble again, but kept his eyes firmly fixed upon the Lord Jesus, the source of spiritual power.

Power in the Old Testament

The power of God, which is given through the Holy Spirit, did not originate at Pentecost. It was the anointing of the Spirit that brought power to the leaders of ancient Israel. Scripture bears witness to the Spirit of God being received by men and women such as Abraham, Moses, Joshua, the Judges, the godly Kings of Israel and Judah, as well as the prophets and spiritual leaders of the nation. The outstanding difference at Pentecost was that the Holy Spirit came upon *the whole body of believers*; the power was available for all, not just the leaders of the nation.

The Bible testifies to the power of God underlying the universe. He is the Creator and Sustainer of all things. He holds the nations in his hands and weighs the mountains on scales (Isaiah 40:12–15). 'What is man that you are mindful of him?' asks the Psalmist (8:4). When man is faced with insuperable problems, and acknowledges his own weakness and utter dependence upon God, the power of God is available to him.

This is demonstrated many times in Scripture such as when Jehoshaphat was facing overwhelming odds and led the whole nation in prayer acknowledging, 'Power and might are in your hand, and no one can withstand you' (2 Chron. 20:6). His prayer reached the height of faith, 'We have no power to face this vast army that is attacking us. We do not know what to do, but our eyes are upon you' (20:12).

Similarly, when Hezekiah was faced by the mighty army of Assyria he encouraged the people by declaring, 'there is a greater power with us than with him. With him is only the arm of flesh, but with us is the Lord our God to help us and to fight our battles' (2 Chron. 32:7–8). From earliest times, it was recognised that when the power of God came upon individuals they were enabled to do things beyond their human strength. It was then that the glory was given to God for the mighty deeds.

Jesus bestowed power on his disciples to enable them to carry out his commands. He gave the twelve 'power and authority to drive out all demons and to cure diseases, and he sent them out to preach the kingdom of God and to heal the sick' (Luke 9:1-2).

The Great Commission concluded with the promise of Jesus to be with his followers always, to the end of the age. It was this promise, and the evidence of the presence of Jesus with them, that gave great boldness to the witness of the first generation of apostles and believers. They actually experienced the power of Jesus working through them.

When the Holy Spirit came upon the whole company of believers at Pentecost, he came in power and gave them spiritual gifts. The Spirit enabled them to speak the word 'with great boldness ... to heal and perform miraculous signs and wonders' through the Name of Jesus (Acts 4:29-30). The power to perform miracles was one of the spiritual gifts listed by Paul in 1 Corinthians 12. Paul clearly links this gift with the exercise of faith and belief in the Lord Jesus (Gal. 3:5). According to Paul's teaching, all the spiritual gifts were given for the purpose of building up the church and strengthening the faith of believers (Eph. 4:12).

In Mary's Song of Praise she gave thanks that the power of God had scattered the proud and mighty and had lifted up the humble, the poor and the weak (Luke 1:51-53). Paul expressed this as a spiritual principle when he noted that the power of Christ is 'made perfect in weakness ... when I am weak, then I am strong.' (2 Cor. 12:9-10). He added, 'We are weak in him, yet by God's power we will live with him to serve you' (2 Cor. 13:4).

A mark of discipleship throughout the Bible was that true men and women of God always gave the glory to him, none was retained for themselves. Paul spoke about, 'what Christ has accomplished through me . . . by the power of signs and miracles, through the power of the Spirit' (Romans 15:18-19). 'My message and my preaching were not with wise and persuasive words, but with a demonstration of the Spirit's power, so that your faith might not rest on men's wisdom, but on God's power' (1 Cor. 2:4). Signs and miracles in Paul's teaching should point to God's power and should not be thought of as containing any power in themselves.

Signs of Jesus' teaching were important evidence of the power of the Father at work. Jesus nevertheless recognised that signs did not necessarily lead unbelievers to faith in God. It was immediately after the 'feeding of the 4,000' that the Pharisees and Sadducees came to Jesus and demanded a miraculous sign. His response was that the only sign they would be given was that of Jonah, which was a straight call to repentance (Matt. 16:1-4). Jesus, in fact, gave many signs during his ministry but, as John noted, 'Even after Jesus had done all these miraculous signs in their presence, they still would not believe in him' (John 12:37).

Jesus refused to give signs to the faithless. He knew that without faith in God, even when people saw a demonstration of his power, they would not believe. Their eyes were blinded by unbelief and only faith could give them sight. Many times Jesus refused to give signs to the unbelieving leaders in his day (Matt. 12:38, Mark 8:11; Luke 11:16; John 6:30). His response was 'the work of God is this: to believe in the one he has sent' (John 6:29).

Jesus often appealed to those he had healed, *not* to tell others as he did not want people to follow him merely because they saw the miraculous power he exercised. The gift of 'miraculous powers' to which Paul refers in 1 Corinthians 12:10 was not intended to be a tool of evangelism to convince unbelievers, but to be part of the spiritual equipment of the body of Christ. There is great danger in the use of miraculous

110

power in the presence of unbelievers. They may well be convinced and become believers, committing their lives to Christ, but the result is usually to produce shallow Christians with no depth of faith. When miracles are used in evangelism, the effect is similar to Jesus' parable of the sower where the seed falls on stony ground. It sprang up immediately but the soil was poor, the roots did not go deep enough and the sun soon scorched the young plants (Luke 8). Those who become Christians as a result of miracles are like the crowd who followed Jesus for 'the loaves' – they are 'rice Christians' who simply want the goodies and whose faith never reaches maturity.

Jesus warned that miraculous power can be misused and should not be regarded as a test of true discipleship. He said that many would come to him and say, 'Lord, Lord, did we not prophesy in your name, and in your name drive out demons and perform many miracles?' (Matt. 7:22). Jesus said he would respond by disclaiming as 'evil doers' those who were using the power of his name for their own glorification.

Even those who became believers and received the Holy Spirit could be guilty of misusing the gifts. Simon the Sorceror, who was converted through Philip's ministry, was one who tried to buy the miraculous power of the Holy Spirit. He was a man who had boasted that he was someone great and was known as the 'Great Power', because of the magic he had learned and the sorcery he practised, but now he wanted even more power so that when he laid hands on men and women they would receive the Holy Spirit (Acts 8:10). But Peter perceived that his heart was not right even though he claimed to be a believer. His motives were wrong in asking for spiritual power and it was denied him.

When the disciples asked Jesus about the signs of the end of the age, the first thing he gave was a warning about deception, 'Watch out that no one

111

deceives you' (Matt. 24:4). He repeated his warnings about false Christs and false prophets saying that they would, 'deceive even the elect – if that were possible' (Matt. 24:24). Paul, in his second letter to the Thessalonians, warned the church that with the coming of the 'man of lawlessness', all kinds of counterfeit miracles, signs and wonders would appear and many would be deceived (2 Thess. 2:9).

But signs and wonders are not to be avoided for fear that they may be wrong, otherwise we may cut ourselves off from some of the precious things God wants to give us, and prevent him using our lives as he wishes to do. One of the gifts of the Spirit is the 'gift of discernment' which enables the believer to distinguish between the genuine and the counterfeit. Jesus promised that the true believer would know his voice as surely as the sheep recognised the voice of their own shepherd. Jesus also said that signs and wonders would accompany the preaching of the Gospel (Mark 16:17). Paul said, 'The things that mark an apostle – signs, wonders and miracles – were done among you with great perseverance' (2 Cor. 12:12), and the book of Acts gives many examples of the apostles' demonstrating this power (Acts 2:43 and 5:12). Genuine spiritual power is available for all believers and may be discerned in the lives of those who are in a right relationship with God.

Underlying Principles

There are four outstanding principles which are apparent in the exercise of spiritual power.

The first is that the power of God is only made perfect in *our powerlessness*. Paul discovered this, and so he actually boasted in his weakness. When we realise that we can do nothing for ourselves, and we are prepared to acknowledge our powerlessness, then God can do mighty deeds because we allow him to do so. Whenever we think we can do things in our own strength, our self-confidence acts as a blockage to the power of God. If we really want to see the power of God in our lives, our confidence has to be in him and not in the flesh.

Linked with this is the fact that God's power must *glorify God*. It is not given to elevate individuals, but to bring glory, honour and praise to God. That is why the spiritual gifts are given for use within the church. They should not be regarded as individual possessions but as spiritual gifts belonging to the whole Christian community. When the gifts are used rightly in the context of humility and love they build up the church so providing a safeguard for individual believers against vanity and the glorification of self.

Thirdly, the power of God in signs and wonders is *given to believers for believers*, not for unbelievers. It is not intended to be used for evangelism. In fact, there are great dangers when signs and wonders are performed in the presence of unbelievers as Paul and Barnabas found out to their cost – almost at the cost of Paul's life. The two apostles performed a miracle of healing in Lystra, and the people were more impressed with the miracle workers than with the message, and they started to worship Paul and Barnabas as gods. They had great difficulty convincing the crowd that they were mortals just like the rest of humanity and that it was God who should receive the glory (Acts 14:8-20).

Finally, it is a basic principle of New Testament teaching that signs and wonders *follow the preaching of the Gospel*. They should be the natural outcome of the proclamation of the Gospel. When the word of God is faithfully declared by men and women of faith, who are in a right relationship with God, the hearts of both believers and unbelievers are open to receive from God. The power of the Holy Spirit is released among the people, to change lives, to heal, to deliver the oppressed and to bring joy and blessing to the whole company of those present.

Questions

1 In an age when the secular world is obsessed with the paranormal, why are Christians so reluctant to accept the reality of signs and wonders?

2 God's power available to the Church takes many forms. Many Christians value healing as the most desirable gift and the greatest evidence of God's power available to believers. Does this indicate western obsession with physical health and material things?

3 Surveys indicate that the laity have greater confidence in the scriptural basis of Christian faith and belief than the clergy. How do you account for this?

4 Jesus told his disciples to wait in Jerusalem for the power of God to come upon them before setting out to fulfil the Great Commission (Acts 1:4). Does the same principle apply to us today and is there evidence of the Church's obedience in this respect?

5 In the New Testament, power was available to all believers. Is this true today and do you see the evidence in *your* church?

6 Why is it that so often intellectualism and spiritual power appear to be dichotomous?

7 In what ways do you see the power of God expressed today? In this chapter reference has been made to the 'power of God coming down on the people'. What does this mean?

8 In this chapter the underlying principles noted were that God's power appears through 'our powerlessness' and is given to 'glorify God'. Power is given 'to believers for believers' and 'signs follow the preaching of the Gospel'. Can you distiguish any other principles?

Chapter Six

Prophetic Witness

*If you do away with the yoke of oppression, with
the pointing finger and malicious talk, and if you
spend yourselves on behalf of the hungry and
satisfy the needs of the oppressed, then your light
will rise in the darkness, and your night will
become like the noonday.*

Isaiah 58:9–10

Rich Christians

Any definition of prophetic witness must begin with
the ministry of the prophets of ancient Israel. Their
witness in the nation was based on their understanding
of the nature of God and of his requirements for his
people. The prophets believed God to be a God of
justice and of righteousness who required from his
people, behaviour in keeping with justice and
righteousness. In the Name of the Lord, they stood
against oppression, powerlessness, injustice, lies and
deception, poverty, greed and avarice, corruption and
exploitation.

Through the prophets in each generation God
called for right standards of behaviour in the nation.
'Let justice roll on like a river, righteousness like a
never-failing stream!' (Amos 5:24). The prophetic
witness required great courage in standing up against
the rich and the powerful rulers in the nation. They
often put their lives at risk by opposing corrupt and
evil rulers. But the essence of the prophetic witness

was that they cared more for righteousness and truth than they did for their own comfort and safety.

There is no nation today that has a monopoly of righteousness or of unrighteousness. Greed and corruption are worldwide and are characteristics of the general sinfulness of mankind. In some non-western nations corruption and naked aggression are more blatantly obvious, whereas in western nations corruption takes a more sophisticated form and is often hidden within the power structures of massive international corporations, or is institutionalised in social systems that perpetuate disadvantage and protect the privileged. Prophetic witness always involves personal cost and self-sacrifice. In western nations this may involve facing up to scorn, the loss of social status, position and wealth, whereas in non-western nations a prophetic witness may actually cost Christians their lives.

Uganda
This is what happened in Uganda during President Idi Amin's reign of terror. Following the military coup, which he led and which overthrew the civilian government of Prime Minister Obote, Amin systematically eliminated not only his political opponents but also any who opposed his evil and corrupt regime. Thousands suffered torture and brutal murder. Outstanding among the Christians who opposed Amin was Archbishop Luwum, who forthrightly condemned the despotic rule of military dictatorship and, as a consequence, was foully murdered. His death shocked the world and was a reminder that martyrdom is still the ultimate cost of true prophetic witness. The Archbishop suffered martyrdom because the Church had not stood out strongly against the corruption among politicians and businessmen *prior* to the military coup.

Laban Jjumba, a Christian leader in Uganda today, recalls how Uganda had once been the 'jewel in the crown of Africa'; a country blessed with so many resources and riches, but which today is reduced to economic poverty. He sees Uganda as a parable; it was a country which had responded to the Gospel message and where there had been great revivals in the 1950s and 1960s; a country which had been able to take the Gospel to other countries on the continent of Africa and which had grown to be respected throughout the world.

But the Church had gradually lost its prophetic cutting edge and settled for a quiet existence. All seemed well in the country and although the seeds of corruption were being sown and were growing, the Church did not take any notice and did not speak out. The Christians had forgotten their prophetic responsibility for the nation. When Idi Amin came to power, the Church as a whole was unprepared and Christians along with others suffered greatly at his hands. The whole nation became a byword for the violence and corruption which continues to this day. The Church today is divided and has little national influence. Laban sees this as a parable of what can happen to a country which has seen the Lord's blessing but ceases to trust in God, trusting rather in itself and in its own strength. This results in the Church ceasing to be a prophetic people making a witness in the nation.

Northern Nigeria

The behaviour of Christians under persecution can often be a powerful witness to unbelievers. This happened recently in northern Nigeria in a strongly Muslim area. In 1987, in Kaduna province, more than 150 Christian churches were burnt down in Muslim riots against the minority Christian community. The whole Muslim population had been stirred up by Islamic fundamentalists to make 'holy war' against the Christians. During several weeks of public anarchy, the authorities were accused of turning a blind eye to the violence, and many Christians suffered physical abuse and a number were killed.

The reaction of the Christians, as their homes and their churches were burnt to the ground, was quite remarkable. Instead of retaliating, returning violence with violence, they showed great restraint and were obedient to the teaching of Jesus to show love to those who were their enemies, and gentleness to those who persecuted them. This had a remarkable effect upon the Muslim population that produced an even more remarkable consequence. Less than a year later, the first local government elections since the military coup were held. In Kaduna, the province at the centre of the troubles, a Christian chairman was returned, and 14 out of the 19 newly-elected representatives were Christian.

The Islamic leaders were dismayed and the whole Muslim population of the north was amazed, but the simple fact was that the Christians had demonstrated their trustworthiness even under the extremes of persecution. Corruption among politicians in Nigeria is notorious and, in the eyes of non-Christians, the Christians had demonstrated not only the steadfastness of their faith but also their love and forgiveness. Even the Muslims knew that they could trust these men and women to be concerned for the total welfare of the area. Their behaviour had given them the opportunity, through legal and democratic means, to alter the way the area is governed and to establish standards of righteousness in public affairs.

Bribery and corruption are widespread throughout Nigeria; civil servants and officials expect to receive favours from members of the public in return for carrying out their duties. Even simple matters, such as obtaining government permits, visas and passports, or obtaining approval for business transactions, can be subject to long delays unless the officials handling them are suitably rewarded.

At a national conference of Christian leaders from all over Nigeria, held at Port Harcourt in 1988, at which I was present, a significant stand against corruption was taken. One thousand leaders stood and solemnly covenanted to refuse to pay bribes under any circumstances. They pledged themselves to stand for righteousness and to refute all forms of corruption. They did this knowing that it would bring the Church into conflict with the authorities, that it would involve personal suffering and hardship, that it might mean delays in building new churches, impose travel restrictions, present problems in obtaining permission for open-air evangelistic meetings and thus prove a hindrance to the mission of Christ. But their confidence in the Lord was so great that they believed that by standing for righteousness and being prepared to make a prophetic witness publicly to the nation, their God would defend them. They believed strongly that the power of God would overcome the forces of evil if they put their trust in him and refused to follow the ways of the world. They saw the cleansing of the church from corruption as a first step towards cleansing the nation. They took their stand upon the biblical principle that 'righteousness exalts a nation'.

South America

A prophetic witness by Christians against a different form of corruption is that of the church in the Upper Amazon area of Brazil. Here, a stand has been made by Christians against the destruction of the tropical rain forests by rich landowners, who care nothing for the effect upon the environment of their relentless pursuit of wealth. The hardwood trees, many of which are hundreds of years old, are enormously valuable on the world market. But as huge areas of forest are cleared it has a devastating effect upon the land, the environment and the people of the region.

Outstanding among the Christian leaders in the

area was Chico Mendes, who fearlessly stood against the powerful landowners with their private armies knowing them to be ruthless in dealing with any who opposed them or spoke against their exploitation of the poor and the powerless. Mendes was brutally murdered in December 1988. Shortly before his death, when coming out of a prayer meeting where he had been joining with the local Christian community in worship and intercession, he pointed out to a friend a passing car occupied by two gunmen who were shadowing him. He told the friend that the day would come when the gunmen would be ordered to kill him. He refused to cease to make his prophetic witness even though he knew his life to be in danger. Like the prophets of old, he preferred to face death rather than to be unfaithful to the word of God that he was given to proclaim.

There are many strands of Liberation Theology, some strongly bible-based, others more Marxist. Mendes' prophetic stand against greed and exploitation represents the highest tradition of modern Liberation Theology that relates the Gospel to issues in contemporary society and seeks to overcome the might of mammon by the power of the word of the living God, to set the prisoner free and to liberate those held in bondage to corrupt rulers. One of the things that Liberation Theology has shown is that each of us perceives the Gospel from the standpoint of our own environment. Our thinking is inevitably influenced by our social and economic circumstances. Thus the poor will hear the Gospel as 'Good News to the poor' while the wealthy perceive the Gospel as justifying their positions of social privilege and power and will declare 'God wants you rich'.

The poor rejoice in hearing those parts of the Gospel that declare God's intention to put down the mighty from their seat, to overthrow the rich and the powerful and to bring judgment upon the wicked and those who exploit the powerless. They expect to see the Gospel making an impact upon the nation and bringing about radical social change. Liberation theologians do not recognise the division between saving souls and social action that they perceive as a Western distortion of the Gospel. Of course they recognise the necessity for each individual to make a life-changing commitment to Christ but they perceive the individual as being an integral part of society so that once the individual is changed there is an inevitable impact upon society. They do not perceive the individual in isolation from society in the same way as western theologians. Thus for them there is no dichotomy between the impact of the Gospel upon the individual and upon society. Thus the Gospel that brings salvation to each believer also brings about revolutionary social change.

In many parts of South America, the church is playing an active role in politics. The Catholic church, in particular, has taken a courageous stand against corrupt and despotic rulers who have for generations been exploiting the people. The church is clearly identified with the poor. Its leaders have been prepared to champion the cause of the powerless, and many have suffered as a consequence. South America, which is the cradle of Liberation Theology, has also seen the development of base ecclesial communities after the pattern of the New Testament church. These have usually grown out of small groups of believers in house fellowships where the members have fully committed their lives to each other under the Lordship of Jesus and have devoted themselves both to worship and to community action. Christian leaders see this as part of the church's prophetic witness against the greed and avarice of corrupt political leaders and their exploitation of the people.

The church has identified with the poor and the underprivileged in much the same way as Amos identified with the poor in Israel, and warned the rich oppressors that judgment would come upon them. But unlike Amos, who called for repentance and spiritual change in order to bring the nation into a right relationship with God and thereby create relationships of justice in society, the church in South America aims at changing social structures through political initiatives. This inevitably brings upon them the criticism that they are seeking to change society by means of man's ways rather than God's. There are, however, many Christians who would refute this criticism and say that it is an essential part in the outworking of the Gospel to be actively involved in political initiatives which lead to fundamental changes in society and to the establishment of social justice.

South Africa
This would certainly be the attitude of many Christian leaders in South Africa who see apartheid as an affront to everything for which the Gospel stands. They see it as one of the most evil forms of injustice and exploitation in the modern world, whereby millions of men, women and children are condemned to poverty and powerlessness simply on the basis of their racial origins. They see no hope of change other than through political initiatives. They point to the historical fact that those who hold absolute power in society never willingly surrender their position of privilege.

Many Christians under these circumstances are prepared even to condone the use of force in order to overthrow a corrupt regime and to establish justice for the oppressed. This was the position taken by the worldwide Anglican church at the 1988 Lambeth Conference. It is a position that has long been held by the World Council of Churches whose support of black nationalist groups in South Africa has been regarded as controversial by many Christians, and as a courageous prophetic witness by others. It is, however, an essential characteristic of prophetic witness that it *is* controversial! Some will hate it and some will applaud it. The prophets were certainly not universally popular, and although the poor heard Jesus gladly the rulers sought to crucify him.

The crucial question is what attitude should Christians take when faced with either a blatantly evil regime or even a democratically elected government which is acting unrighteously. Does the church have a duty to speak out against unrighteousness, corruption, deception, exploitation and injustice? Certainly, the biblical prophets took it to be an essential part of their ministry, for which they were answerable to God, to speak against such things in the Name of the Lord.

Kenya
Bishop David Gitari did just that in 1987 at the time of the registration for the first General Elections in Kenya since the military coup. He claims to be an expository preacher 'sharing an understanding of the historical and spiritual context of different Bible passages and letting them come alive in the modern situation'. The two main issues of controversy at the time of this registration were the announcement that only people who had been enrolled as paid-up members of the Kenya African National Union (KANU) would be eligible to vote in the national elections, and that the election would not be conducted as a secret ballot but by voters publicly standing behind the candidate of their choice, a system clearly open to corruption.

At a civic service, attended by many national leaders in Nyere in June 1987, David Gitari chose to preach on Daniel 6 where the prime-minister-designate of the Persian Empire was removed from his position for conspiracy, although the truth eventually triumphed. The outcry was immediate and loud as the leaders presumed that comparisons were being made with their own positions in Kenya while, at the same time, denying that there was any parallel!

Bishop Gitari was not on his own in the firing line for long. As the election progressed, church leaders continued to speak out against the injustices in the proposed system. The outcome of the controversy was not as the government had expected. They were unable to destroy the credibility of the Church, but rather the reverse happened. The people began flocking to the churches in Kenya and preachers drew greater crowds than the political leaders. The people saw the Church standing against injustice and speaking the truth even in the face of the opposition of political rulers. The prophetic stand of the Church in Kenya has been a major contributory factor in the spiritual revival presently sweeping the nation.

Poor Christians

In the West today there is probably no area that more clearly reveals the division in the life of the churches than that of prophetic witness. The witness of the prophets in Scripture always concerned matters of both public and personal morality as part of their concern for the spiritual health of the nation. To the prophets, both kinds of morality were aspects of loyalty to God – the one being worked out in the personal life of the individual, and the other being worked out in family life, in the community and in the nation.

Western Christians appear to have lost sight of this wholeness of the biblical prophetic witness. Theological divisions have created a kind of tunnel vision so that only certain narrow aspects of the out-working of the Gospel are seen. The emphasis is either upon the personal or the societal implications of the Gospel, rarely upon both.

Social Morality

It is the liberal churches that see the need for the Gospel to make an impact on every aspect of public life and social organisation. They believe that Christians should be involved in the political process at both local and national levels; that the Church should be standing with the poor and the powerless; that Christians should be speaking out against exploitation and injustice wherever it is found; that Christians should be supporting minority groups, and showing a concern for those who are the casualties of modern urban industrial systems. *But* they see the role of the Church not simply in terms of the provision of social first aid to the needy, but in terms of effecting changes in the unjust social systems that create poverty and social disadvantage.

It is the liberal churches that are the most active in inner-city areas where poverty and inequality are most apparent and where immigrants and minority groups abound. These were once areas of mission for evangelicals, but the latter have largely withdrawn to the suburbs and more salubrious areas thus leaving the field mainly in the hands of those whom evangelicals regard as purveyors of a 'social gospel'.

In Britain many liberal churches are actively involved in work with racial minorities composed of immigrant workers from the Caribbean, from Africa and from India and Pakistan, who have settled in inner-city areas. Many Christians are actively involved in voluntary work, teaching English to non-English speaking groups, running youth clubs, playgroups, and organising work among the elderly. Many churches also use their premises for work among the unemployed or as drop-in centres for vagrants, and for work among young drug addicts.

The liberal churches are also active in many movements of a sociopolitical nature, such as campaigns for minority rights or peace movements. They see nothing incongruous in Christians making their witness alongside secular humanists in movements seeking to promote justice, social equality or the improvement of living conditions for the poor.

There is a quality of selflessness in the service offered by many so-called liberal Christians in inner-city areas. They give themselves unstintingly to the work, sharing in the lifestyle of the local people and the social deprivation of the area. They see their work as part of the prophetic witness of the Church in self-giving without seeking reward.

They would claim to be more concerned with the values of the Kingdom than with building the Church as an institution. They have rejected the concept of 'rice Christianity' or what they see as 'nineteenth-century evangelical soup Christianity' which offered food to the poor provided they came to church or accepted tracts. Their primary concern is with the love of Christ in action in the community. They see this as a value in itself regardless of whether or not it brings conversions and increases the membership of the Church.

Personal Morality
By contrast, traditionally evangelical churches throughout the West have stressed the prime importance of personal standards of behaviour and personal morality. This stemmed from the theological emphasis of evangelicals upon the necessity of conversion as a personal experience, and the conviction that it was the personal relationship of the individual to God that was the key to holiness. This concern of evangelicals with the primacy of conversion and personal faith often overlooked the physical circumstances in which people were living.

Evangelicals would say that they are not unconcerned with social conditions but that their paramount concern is with the spiritual well-being of each individual because they believe that changed individuals will change social conditions. Thus they see the main need as being to establish standards of righteousness in the individual as being the only effective way of establishing standards of righteousness in society.

In Britain, the 1980s have seen a new mood among evangelicals, particularly younger ones, that has brought about a greater concern for public morality, and is a reaction against traditional evangelical separatism. Evangelicals today are active in many spheres of public life, particularly in matters relating to personal morality, such as the family, marriage and the welfare of children.

Many British evangelicals have been carrying their witness into the political sphere, particularly on such matters as the campaign against abortion and the campaign to 'Keep Sunday Special' – to preserve the British Sunday as a day of rest. Evangelicals have also been active in the sphere of education, particularly in campaigning for a return to a stronger biblical emphasis in religious education as a counter to religious syncretism, multi-faith education and teaching on the occult.

Evangelicals see their prophetic witness in terms of promoting higher standards of personal morality and spirituality. They believe that this is the most effective way of raising standards of public morality, and promoting the spiritual health of the nation.

Tunnel Vision
The tunnel vision referred to at the beginning of this section is limited not only by theological differences and different attitudes to society, but also by the lack of a worldwide vision of the purposes of God. Evangelicals think in terms of personal change, and liberals think in terms of social change, but neither addresses the wider issues of international injustice that is institutionalised in western society. Christians of all churches occasionally speak out against apartheid and contribute to disaster funds, such as famine relief

and flood relief, but western Christians rarely tackle the basic issues. The western churches are too closely identified with western culture and the economic and social structures of the western world to be able to mount an effective critique or to initiate policies of change.

The western churches do not have a history of radicalism; from the time of the conversion of Constantine they have usually been associated with the ruling party rather than with those who challenge the authorities. The heritage of the western churches is essentially conservative. They have rarely been identified with the poor; even Luther supported the German Princes in putting down the Peasants Revolt.

In some European nations, the Church is identified with a particular political party and is supported by a tax levied by the State. Under such circumstances Christians are hardly likely to espouse radical policies that might undermine the authority of the State from which they benefit. The same principle applies to all the western churches who depend for their support upon the affluence of their nations.

Much of the wealth of the western nations is derived from multinational corporations, who often protect their own interests by exploiting the poorer nations, and have a monopoly of industrial processes and production which limits the competition of the developing nations. The western nations also control the world banking system and although loans are given to the developing nations, high interest rates and the conditions under which loans are granted ensure that the western nations maintain their riches and the other nations are kept in poverty. It is these basic injustices that Christians in the 'two-thirds world' deeply resent, and wonder why their brothers and sisters in the western churches do not speak out against them and seem unwilling to make a prophetic witness in line with biblical Christianity.

The fact is that the western churches are too closely identified with the economic and social systems of the western nations because most of their members are drawn from the middle classes and they derive their wealth from the present system. Most western Christians are not even aware of the plight of the poor and do not recognise their responsibility for ensuring that the Church brings a prophetic witness to bear upon those who hold political and economic power.

Gustavo Gutiérrez in *A Theology of Liberation*, refers to the dehumanising effects of poverty in some parts of Latin America. He says, 'Poor people are by-products of the system under which we live and for which we are responsible. Poor people are ones who have been shunted to the sidelines of our socio-cultural world.' It is for this reason that Gutiérrez concludes, 'That is why the poverty of the poor is not a summons to alleviate their plight with acts of generosity but rather a compelling obligation to fashion an entirely different social order.' Western Christians cannot excuse their lack of prophetic action to alleviate the plight of the poor in third world countries by claiming a lack of knowledge of the situation. Ignorance is no excuse today; the documentary information is freely available but most Christians either do not want to know or simply do not care. It is also not a valid excuse to say that nothing can be done. The Church has an obligation to take a prophetic stand on the side of the materially poor and the oppressed for this is part of the biblical heritage at the heart of the Christian faith. To keep silent is to become aligned with the oppressors and to share in their guilt.

Historical Perspectives

The First World War was a watershed experience for Europe that shattered the complacency of the nations and paved the way for the radical social changes that have taken place during the rest of the century. The period between the two world wars was a time of fundamental change in the thinking of the masses in regard to the social order, the rights of the individual and the place of authority in society. The demand for equality and the franchise of women were part of the radical social changes that began in the 1920s and have gathered momentum in successive decades.

Radical social changes were introduced at the same time as secular humanism was spreading in the West and the authority of Scripture was being challenged by the widespread teaching of biblical criticism in the theological colleges. This inevitably added to the uncertainties of the age in regard to the authority of the moral law that lay at the root of the social order that had been stable in most western nations for centuries. Throughout the West, the 1920s and 1930s were a time of great social and industrial upheaval that witnessed the years of poverty and economic depression following the crash of 1929.

It was in this period that the divide between evangelical and liberal began to open up. In Britain, it coincided with the secularisation of the Labour movement that largely occurred during this period. The roots of the radical political movement out of which the Labour party and the trade unions grew in the nineteenth century were strongly linked with the Gospel. Gospel preachers who emphasised the prophetic word of God concerning the conditions of the poor and the plight of the urban industrial peasants of the nineteenth century were among the founders of the British Labour movement. Many of the radical politicians in the Liberal party in the late nineteenth century and early twentieth century were lay preachers such as Lloyd George, the longest serving male prime minister of this century!

The Great Divide

As the Labour movement moved farther away from its biblical and spiritual roots, the gap between evangelical and liberal Christians widened. It was a two-way process of polarisation with radical Christian thinkers not only challenging traditional concepts of authority in the State, but also challenging traditional attitudes to Scripture and the more conservative aspects of the Gospel that gave support to the position of the rich and the more privileged in society.

Those Christian thinkers who were more conservatively inclined tended to react against the new radical ideas, both sociopolitical and theological. They emphasised the infallibility of Scripture as the divinely inspired word of God, and rejected most aspects of modern biblical criticism. They further reacted by moving away from the social expression of the Christian faith that had been a major characteristic of Victorian churches of all denominations.

The emphasis of evangelicals began to centre exclusively upon conversion and the spiritual needs of man. Many evangelical preachers said that their only interest was in 'saving souls', thus many evangelical churches would have nothing to do with 'social' activities including youth clubs, dances, fetes and fayres, sewing meetings, drama groups or any other non-spiritual activities, all of which were considered to be 'worldly'. The only things allowed were prayer meetings, Bible study groups, midweek and Sunday services, revivalist meetings plus tract evangelism in the streets, and door-to-door evangelism around the houses.

In the 1970s, the tide began to turn with the widespread recognition of the declining moral state of the nation. Evangelicals began to realise that their withdrawal from the sociopolitical scene had allowed the permissive legislation of the 1950s and 1960s to go through unchallenged, and this had resulted in fundamental changes in society through changes to the law on divorce, abortion, witchcraft, homosexuality and censorship. In the same period, Christians in the liberal churches also began showing a greater awareness of the moral and spiritual barrenness in the nation. This coincided with a general disillusionment with the achievements of the welfare state, and with a decline of confidence in the Labour movement to produce the kind of social Utopia that had been the motivating ideal of the early Labour movement. Selfishness and greed characterised all sections of society, rich and poor alike, in the 1970s and 1980s and many liberal Christians began to turn increasingly to a greater emphasis upon spiritual values, and to be increasingly open to evangelism.

Bridging the Divide
It may be that later generations will see a wider significance in the rise of the Charismatic movement throughout the 1970s and 1980s. This movement penetrated both the liberal and evangelical sectors of the church, and has undoubtedly contributed to new spiritual life in the church. Part of this new spiritual activity has been associated with the exercise of the gift of prophecy. This has led to a new emphasis on listening to God and a desire to know what the Spirit is saying to the churches today. There is some evidence that this has led to a greater concern for the prophetic witness of the church in society, particularly in relation to matters of social morality and social caring. Nevertheless most of the prophetic words heard in Charismatic churches relate to matters concerning the life of the fellowship or to personal needs. Very few of these 'prophecies' have the kind of edge that Amos would recognise as being worthy of the introduction 'Thus says the Lord. . .!'

The rise of the Charismatic movement has not changed the basic perspective of the western churches.

The 1980s have been a decade that has seen some of the worst disasters since the beginning of recorded history, with millions dying of starvation through drought, famine and plagues of locusts. Millions more have been suffering from malnutrition and diseases, multitudes have been made homeless from natural disasters, from flood, earthquakes, mudslides and storms, as well as through the horrors of modern warfare. Yet despite all this human suffering, there has been no worldwide prophetic action initiated by the rich and powerful churches of the West. Despite the influence they exercise within their own nations, it is notable that the most prophetic action on behalf of the starving multitudes in central and eastern Africa following the Ethiopian Famine Appeal came from the pop star Bob Geldof and not from the churches. Millions of pounds were raised by young people through pop concerts in all the western nations. It would appear that prophetic witness no longer comes from the Church. The songs of radical protest sung by rock musicians are however, a poor substitute for the prophetic word of God to the nations.

Biblical Witness

The message of the prophets was derived from their understanding of the nature of God. It was because they believed God to be a God of justice and righteousness that the prophets were able to demand justice and righteousness from his people. Hence Jeremiah declared, '"Let him who boasts boast about this: that he understands and knows me, that I am the Lord, who exercises kindness, justice and righteousness on earth, for in these things I delight", declares the Lord' (Jeremiah 9:24).

Isaiah also spoke of God as a God of justice, and he linked this with God's love and mercy and his desire to show compassion to his people despite their sinfulness and rebellion. 'Yet the Lord longs to be gracious to you; he rises to show you compassion. For the Lord is a God of justice' (Isaiah 30:18).

Justice and Righteousness

The prophets saw no contradiction between the love and compassion of God, and his justice, even though the latter sometimes meant bringing judgment upon a sinful people. The reason for this lies in the Hebrew understanding of justice, which is in sharp contrast to the western view of justice. The western concept of law and justice is based upon the Roman concept of retributive justice, making the punishment fit the crime, whereas, for the Hebrew, justice lay in right relationships. The just man was one who was in a right relationship with God and with his neighbours. The Hebrew prophets saw that God in his love and mercy longed to have compassion on the penitent sinner, and to restore him to a right relationship with himself. They saw that rebellion and wrongdoing estranged men and women from God. Evil deeds broke the harmonious relationships which are based upon love and trust. This is what Isaiah meant when he said that God was looking for right relationships with, and among, his people, but he found only violence. 'He looked for justice, but saw bloodshed; for righteousness, but heard cries of distress' (Isaiah 5:7).

Justice and righteousness, which are interchangable terms throughout the Bible, both stemming from the same root, are central to the message of the prophets. In declaring the word of God to the nation, they spoke against idolatry, injustice, oppression, adultery, violence and murder, lies and deceit, greed and avarice, and many other aspects of sinful behaviour. But, basically, their message always came back to the central theme that the nation, which was in a covenant relationship with God, had turned away from him, and broken the harmonious relationship of love and

134

trust that should exist between God and his people. There was no excuse because they knew his word, and they had deliberately chosen to disobey and thereby turn their backs upon the living God. The right relationship could only be restored through the repentance of the people and the forgiveness of God.

Just as unrighteous behaviour caused the breakdown in relationships between God and his people, so in the same way it broke relationships between men and women. The prophets declared that right relationships were broken by greed and exploitation, by jealousy, by lies and deception and by violent and unloving behaviour. Such behaviour was rebellion against God, for when anyone sinned against his neighbour he not only broke a human relationship but also the relationship with God. Hence Amos could speak about God's anger with those who 'trample the needy and do away with the poor of the land' (Amos 8:4). He saw the way the rich and powerful were misusing their positions in the nation to oppress the poor and the powerless, 'You turn justice into bitterness and cast righteousness to the ground . . . you hate the one who reproves in court and despise him who tells the truth . . . you trample on the poor . . . you oppress the righteous and take bribes' (Amos 5:7–12).

Jeremiah spoke in similar terms against those who oppressed the powerless. 'They have grown rich and powerful and have grown fat and sleek. Their evil deeds have no limit; they do not plead the case of the fatherless to win it, they do not defend the rights of the poor' (Jeremiah 5:27–28).

The prophets believed that God identified with those who were the victims of oppression. God is always on the side of the poor. Isaiah expresses the indignation of God in the face of gross injustice and naked aggression, '"What do you mean by crushing my people and grinding the faces of the poor?" declares the Lord, the Lord Almighty' (Isaiah 3:15).

135

Light and Salt
God expected his people to care for one another as he cared for them. In fact, he had called Israel for the special purpose of revealing his nature, his truth and his purposes to all the nations. They were to bring God's 'salvation to the ends of the earth' (Isaiah 49:6), and they were to be a 'light for the Gentiles, to open eyes that are blind, to free captives from prison and to release from the dungeon those who sit in darkness' (Isaiah 42:6-7). Thus the mission of the people of God was to bring light, liberty and truth to the whole world.

Jesus told his disciples, 'You are the salt of the earth ... you are the light of the world' (Matt. 5:13-14). The salt was to stand against corruption, and symbolised cleansing, while the light symbolised truth. To be salt and light in the world was the task that Jesus gave to his followers. This was essentially the ministry that the prophets have carried out in Israel, and it was this prophetic ministry that was now the inheritance of the church as the people of God.

Underlying Principles

The outstanding principle to emerge from this chapter is that of *justice*. It is surely of vital importance for Christians to understand justice in its biblical context of right relationships; i.e. right relationships between people and God and right relationships with each other. The biblical view is that the first step towards harmonious relationships at the human level, is the establishment of a right relationship with God. The teaching of Scripture also includes the fact of God's concern not simply with individuals, but also for each nation and for the whole of mankind. The nature of God is just, and he expects right standards of behaviour from both individuals and nations. He longs to see justice 'roll down like a river and righteousness like a never-failing stream'. God hates every form of injustice and oppression. He is always against those who misuse their power, privilege and resources to oppress others.

A second principle is the *need for a whole Gospel*. The vision of most people is limited by both time and circumstances. We tend to see everything in terms of our own personal experience, which makes it difficult to stand outside a situation and see the wider purposes of God that are being worked out globally, and over the course of centuries. Our vision is partial and this affects our perception of truth, so we tend to emphasise one aspect of the Gospel such as the need for personal salvation or the need for liberating the poor and the oppressed. Scripture bears witness to the fact that salvation is by faith alone, but that faith is expressed in deeds. Love and self-sacrifice are the marks of the true believer.

A third principle is the teaching of the New Testament that believers are to be *salt and light in the world*. Christians are not expected to live in isolation from the world. The promise of Jesus was to keep his followers *in* the world and to be with them wherever they were sent. Jesus prayed to the Father, 'My prayer is not that you take them out of the world but that you protect them from the evil one' (John 17:15). Jesus' teaching also makes it clear that he wants his followers to be 'separated' from the world – to be in the world but not of it. They had to be in the world, although spiritually separated, in order to exercise a spiritual influence. The function of salt is to stand against corruption and to cleanse; while light symbolises the responsibility of Christians to radiate truth by reflecting Jesus, the Light of the World.

Questions

1 The witness of the prophets was always radical and in opposition to established religion. Is the Church inevitably conservative?

2 Is the dichotomy between the personal morality of evangelicals and the social morality of liberals giving way to a new prophetic vision of the purposes of God that goes beyond personal and national interests?

3 Discuss the biblical use of the terms 'justice' and 'righteousness' and apply these concepts to today.

4 Are the prophets of today in secular institutions rather than in the Church? What should the Church in the West be doing to alleviate poverty and oppression in the Third World?

5 Under the Old Covenant, God raised up individual prophets to speak to the nation. Under the New Covenant, the Holy Spirit enabled every believer to prophesy (1 Cor. 14). It was God's intention that the Church should be the prophet to the nations. Are there signs of this being fulfilled today?

6 There is a new interest in prophecy today, but is this simply the desire to hear from God to meet personal and fellowship needs rather than a concern for wider issues?

7 Jesus said his disciples were to be salt and light (Matt. 5:13–16). In what ways is your local church salt and light in the neighbourhood? And what about your own discipleship?

8 The principles underlying prophetic witness appear to be 'justice', 'a need for a whole Gospel' and the 'need to be salt and light in the world'. Can you outline any more?

Chapter Seven

Community Consciousness

Once you were not a people, but now you are the people of God

1 Peter 2:10

Rich Christians

East Africa

Christianity has been in East Africa for well over a hundred years, and there has been a great deal of missionary activity among the Masai tribe since the middle of this century. Schools and hospitals were founded among the Masai, but there were very few converts to the Christian faith. As a tribe, they were very resistant to any ideas coming in from outside. It took considerable effort even to persuade them to allow their children to attend school, or the sick to go to mission hospitals. Resistance to the Gospel appeared to be even stronger, and many missionaries reported that it was impossible to talk to the Masai about God. Mission policy was directed towards establishing relationships of trust, building more schools and hospitals to enable the people to read and to improve their social environment. The policy included involving the people in social activities so that they could provide for their own development, including erecting buildings for worship, and then eventually one day, maybe in future generations, the Masai might see the value of Christianity and come to believe in the missionaries' God.

One man who grew impatient of waiting for the Masai to become open to the Gospel was Vincent Donovan. Writing about his experience in *Christianity Rediscovered* (SCM 1982), he tells how he began to question the traditional mission policy of slipping the Gospel in on the back of community service, and to ask why they were so resistant to the Gospel. He recognised that they had strong close-knit community ties, were a nomadic rather than a settled people, and he also knew that they were essentially a religious people although dominated by witch doctors, fear of evil spirits and traditional animistic beliefs, so he wondered why it was considered impossible to talk to them about God. He determined to try a direct approach, and spoke to one of the headmen telling him that his purpose in coming from a far-off land was not simply to be involved in schools and hospitals, but to talk to the people about God. To his great surprise, the old man replied, 'If that is the reason you came, why did you wait so long to tell us about this? Who can refuse to talk about God?'

The headman and the elders from three neighbouring kraals agreed that he could hold meetings to talk about spiritual things with all the people on a weekly basis, early in the morning, and he was able to make similar arrangements with other villages throughout the region.

He found that in presenting the Gospel he had to do a lot of 'unlearning' to divest it of so many western cultural influences that he had previously taken for granted. He started by asking questions to discover what the people believed, before sharing his own faith. In this way he began from where they were, which was particularly necessary because there were many words missing from their language which he would normally have used to describe basic Christian concepts. He also found that his own thinking was frequently challenged, and that his understanding of

God and his purposes was deepened by the questions asked and the thoughts expressed.

Once he had discovered that their understanding of God was essentially that of a tribal God, he realised that the right starting point was to talk about Abraham and the Israelite tribes, and then to go on to show how the Israelites understanding grew and they came to know God as the one and only true God, Creator of the universe and of all mankind. This stimulated the Masai's interest and their desire to know the 'One High God', and opened the way for him to tell them how God had sent Jesus so that he could be known by all people.

At the end of a year of these regular meetings, he felt the time had come for them to make a commitment and to show this by being baptised. He had shared with them all the essentials of the Gospel; there had been a positive response and he was able to recognise many true believers among them. He spoke to the headman of one of the villages about this, but pointed out that it was a serious step that should not be taken lightly; each one had to make a personal commitment. The response of the old man made him realise the extent to which he himself was still interpreting the Gospel in a western individualistic culture. Donovan recalls the incident as follows:

'I stood in front of the assembled community and began: "This old man sitting here has missed too many of our instruction meetings. He was always out herding cattle. He will not be baptised with the rest. These two on this side will be baptised because they always attended, and understood very well what we talked about. So did this young mother. She will be baptised. But that man there has obviously not understood the instructions. And that lady there has scarcely believed the Gospel message. They cannot be baptised. And this warrior has not shown enought effort . . ."

141

'The old man, Ndangoya, stopped me politely but firmly, "Padri, why are you trying to break us up and separate us? During the whole year that you have been teaching us, we have talked about these things when you were not here, at night around the fire. Yes, there have been lazy ones in this community. But they have been helped by those with much energy. There are stupid ones in the community, but they have been helped by those who are intelligent. Yes, there are ones with little faith in this village, but they have been helped by those with much faith. Would you turn out and drive off the lazy ones and the ones with little faith and the stupid ones? From the first day I have spoken for these people. And I speak for them now. Now, on this day one year later, I can declare for them and for all this community, that we have reached the step in our lives where we can say, We believe."'

Concepts of Commitment

Donovan confesses that until that day he had never thought there could be such a thing as communal belief – he had only ever thought of faith in individualistic terms. Yet the New Testament clearly teaches the value of Christian community. Paul exhorted the Galatians to 'carry each other's burdens' (6:2) so that the strong could help the weak through their 'common belongingness' in Christ. This concept of Christian community has tended to become lost in the western world through the strong emphasis upon the individual, and the lack of commitment to community

People in non-western nations who come from tribal backgrounds have a much deeper affinity with the Old Testament, and a deeper understanding of the community spirit of the twelve tribes of Israel than westerners. They can understand too how impossible it is to be a Christian in isolation from others, and the necessity of belonging to a Christian community under the headship of Christ.

Gwen Cashmore, a former missionary in Africa, recalls an occasion when she was describing her family to some African women by drawing circles in the sand calling one herself and others her father and her mother. She was concerned at the great amusement this caused until they redrew the circles to overlap to show their concept of family. The Africans in their culture could not see themselves in isolation from their family – the fulfilment of each individual could only be found in the fulfilment of the family or community. This, too, is a basic biblical concept found in both the Old and the New Testaments.

At the Lambeth conference in 1988, the wives of the African Bishops became very upset with the attitude of some of the western wives who were promoting the ordination of women and were trying to impose 'independence' on them and push them to stand up for their 'rights' as women. They had no desire to be seen apart from their husbands and tribes; it was in the family that they found their identity. They could see no value in being out on their own; they saw their greatest value as being part of a wider community. It should be noted that they would have been equally strong against the isolation of their husbands as individuals without reference to their wives, families or communities. The western women were unable to appreciate the concept of the worth of each person as being *within* the community rather than as an individual

The concept of community is endemic to most non-western nations. Tribal solidarity has always been a characteristic of African society that has never been understood by Europeans, who arbitrarily divided up the continent in the period of colonialisation. Hostile tribes and those who had little in common were forced together into administrative units because the European settlers recognised only geographical and political boundaries. Africa today is still suffering from internal strife and division caused by the Europeans. Within the newer nations, tribal identity is still stronger than national identity. The disastrous civil war in Nigeria was an inter-tribal conflict between the Ibo tribe in the south-east, and the Hausa and the Yoruba tribes of northern and western Nigeria.

Nigeria

In Nigeria, among Christian professionals there is a deliberate attempt to bridge the old tribal loyalties that produced so much enmity and division, by inter-tribal friendships and even marriages. It is not that they value racial community less highly than others, but rather that they see Christian community as superseding the old narrow tribal understanding of community. The Gospel has widened their understanding of communal responsibility and loyalty. Their tribal understanding of belongingness, of community solidarity and loyalty under the leadership of elders, and the headship of the tribal chief has taken on a new significance as they have embraced the Gospel. It has moulded their understanding of the church as the body of believers recognising common loyalties and obligations to each other under the headship of Christ.

Their understanding of the Lordship of Christ is not confined to his authority over each one of them as individuals but extends to the Lordship of Christ over each village, each community and over the whole state. It matters to Nigerian Christians *who* is recognised as Lord of their nation. They are resisting strongly the Islamisation of the State and are standing out against the imposition of Sharia (the Islamic law) because they want to see Jesus publicly acknowledged as Lord of Nigeria.

People Groups

Mission policy today is changing in recognition of strong tribal links in many parts of the world. It has recently been recognised that the most effective evangelism takes place within 'people groups' rather than in national or regional campaigns. These are the natural groups in which people find their identity. The Gospel can be communicated most effectively in an atmosphere where people feel comfortable and among those whom they trust. The Gospel is also most readily understood when it is presented within the local culture and by those who are sensitive to local needs and conditions, as well as to the nuances of dialect and language. Often this can most effectively be done by an evangelist from the local tribe. It is surely no coincidence that the rapid spread of the Gospel in many non-western nations has taken place only as the Europeans have withdrawn and the non-western nations have achieved independence. As the Gospel has begun to be indigenised, it is also proving to be a most significant unifying force crossing tribal boundaries.

There are many parts of the non-western world where strong tribal loyalties which have proved to be barriers in the past are now being harnessed for the Gospel. Once the Gospel has begun to penetrate a number of different tribes in a region, common loyalty to Christ supersedes or replaces old tribal hostilities. This is well illustrated by the Batu Bible College, which now has a thousand students training as pastors and evangelists drawn from many different tribes in Indonesia, which, in the past, have fought each other. Although Christians from the different tribal origins are proud of their roots and the beauty of their island heritage, their common loyalty to Christ gives them a wider vision of community.

One of the things that strikes the visitor to Batu is the diverse origins of both students and staff, easily distinguishable by their different physical appearances, and yet the strong bonds of unity which are apparent among them. At 5 a.m. the whole campus is alive with songs of praise and voices uplifted in prayer. The eagerness of students to learn, and their zeal for the Gospel, is to be seen even in their times of relaxation when they simply can't stop praising the Lord. They acknowledge that their diverse tribal origins have enriched their understanding of the Gospel and strengthened the bond of unity through a common loyalty to Christ as their head.

A major development in the second half of the twentieth century throughout the non-western world has been the independence movement. This has had a two-way influence. From one standpoint it has severed the old ties of colonialism and thus, to an extent, it has been a movement of 'de-westernisation' alongside which there has been an emphasis upon heritage and local culture and therefore tribal identities. This has resulted in people discovering a pride in their new nationhood and its distinctiveness from western culture.

This is particularly to be seen among the Chinese people, who take great pride in claiming to be the oldest civilisation in the world. Wherever they are to be found throughout the world, the Chinese have a strong sense of identity. It is very unusual indeed for them to intermarry with the people among whom they settle, and they retain their identity even when they are separated from China by thousands of miles, often still observing ancient customs such as the Chinese New Year.

It is largely due to the indigenisation of the Gospel that the Christian community is growing so fast in China; it is doubtful if this would have happened if Christianity was still seen in its western context. It is, however, not just inside China but among Chinese throughout the world that there is a growing openness to the Gospel. The church in Surabaya, Indonesia, described in Chapter Three, which has grown rapidly to 17,000 in ten years, is almost entirely a Chinese congregation. The Chinese churches in Singapore are also experiencing rapid growth. In 1988, I was in Wesley Methodist Church in Singapore, which has grown rapidly since Chinese pastors replaced Europeans in 1970. At that time, after 90 years of missionary activity, they still had a congregation of only 300, but by 1988 they had increased to 4,000, the vast majority being Chinese. The Chinese bring with them a deep respect for the family, for parents and for each other in the community. Modern society and communism may be destroying some of the old cultural roots such as ancestor worship, but there is still a deep respect for parents – honouring father and mother – and an important understanding of the family and village as community.

When the Gospel was taken round the world from the western nations last century, the culture in which it had thrived in Europe, went with it, even to the extent of western buildings, music and churchmanship. In contrast, many local customs were seen as demonic, or as incompatible with the Gospel, and, in order to become a Christian, many community activities had to be rejected. With the coming of independence, and the move to reassert local culture, some churches are being seen as undesirable western imports while indigenous churches are expanding at a great rate.

Indigenisation
In the Anglican church in Kenya there are moves to recognise local culture, and an attempt is being made to dismantle some of the barriers to the spread of the Gospel, erected by the Europeans who originally founded the church.

At the 1988 Lambeth conference, David Gitari, Bishop of Mount Kenya East, made a successful plea for the revoking of the law prohibiting communion and the baptism of men and their wives coming from a polygamous union, until the extra wives had been put away. This had caused much hardship for the rejected wives where the husband had become Christian, and had proved too strong a barrier to other men who had entered into polygamous marriages before becoming Christians.

David Gitari also called for Africans to rediscover some of their African culture and its beauty, and see if the Church could not become meaningful in the full life of the community. He spoke about the Africans' need for colour in their lives and the difficulties imposed by the Europeans who insist that black is the only appropriate colour for church leaders to wear.

He also spoke about the importance of marriage in African communities. In Kenya, the wedding day comes as a climax of a great deal of community activity that not only brings two people together but also unites two families. The tribal ceremonies that take place prior to the church service are important in establishing the marriage in the eyes of the whole community. But the Church only sees the actual wedding ceremony as being of importance, and has little to do with any other part of the celebrations. On the wedding day, the family of the groom come to collect the bride from her family home. The father of the bride does not give her away, but the father of the groom takes her to the church accompanied by weeping, rejoicing, dancing and singing all the way. Once they reach the church, the vicar takes over and leads a solemn service while the people wait outside containing their joy until it is over and the celebrations can resume after the minor interruption. Unfortunately, the joy of the occasion does not overflow into the religious service and the influence of the Church is not felt in every aspect of community life.

Poor Christians

Individualism

Western society is intensely individualistic. The free-market enterprise that is the conceptual basis of capitalism, produces a competitive society with strong drives to upward social mobility and acquisitiveness. These not only mould social values but also create strong drives to individual achievement. Whey we say, 'someone has done very well for himself' we are thinking in terms of economic advancement and achievement of social status. Riches and social honour are the criteria of achievement in western society. The poor are either the objects of scorn or of charity. An achievement-oriented society places little value upon communal ideals, and maximum value on individual achievement.

The Church, far from standing in contrast to secular society, tends to reflect the dominant values of western society. Most church congregations are middle-class and reflect middle-class values. One of the reasons for this is that in Western society, middle-class values are highly regarded and have come to be equated with respectability, honesty and morality, and therefore 'righteousness' is identified with middle-class behaviour patterns. The Church is seen to be the custodian of morality and tends to reflect those values which are closely identified with the middle-classes. But a major ethic of the middle-class is 'individualism' and this too has strong links with religion, particularly with the Protestant work ethic which grew out of the Reformation with its strong emphasis upon individual responsibility, salvation by faith and stewardship in individual accountability.

Fragmentation of Community
With this concentration on the individual in both church and society, there has been a distinct move away from community values and the consequent breakdown of such community spirit as did exist. Whereas we see that the Church as community is replacing traditional, tribal community in the non-

western nations, this concept is very rarely to be found in western society. Christian communities did exist in the past among Europeans as is evidenced by the Amish who settled in America and who continue to retain their eighteenth-century lifestyle within a religious framework. Community also existed in feudal societies of past centuries in most countries of Europe. In those societies, the Church played a significant role and was important in holding the community together but as the twin forces of urbanisation and industrialisation advanced, the community was fragmented, and individualisation was promoted. Both right-wing and left-wing political systems have self-interest at heart, the former concentrates upon the profit-motive and individual gain, while the latter rejects feudalism and servanthood as 'bourgeois' and encourages individuals to take their rights.

The whole of western society is founded upon a belief in the ultimate value of the individual and therefore emphasises individual freedom and individual rights. This has been a major force in the break-up of the extended family, and consequently of community life. Family ties and loyalties have given way to the self-interest of each individual so that the western concept of the family does not include the wider family of several generations with grandparents, uncles, aunts and cousins, but simply focuses upon the small nuclear unit of husband and wife and their progeny. The nuclear family usually exists in isolation from other relatives both geographically and socially and with a weakening code of morality affecting sexual behaviour. Marriage breakdown has increasingly weakened even the nuclear family, and given further impetus to the fragmentation of community and individuation of western society.

The breakdown of family life in society has had a major effect on church life throughout the western nations. Whereas at the beginning of the twentieth century most church congregations included whole families of three or four generations, often very large families, today by contrast there are few congregations where there are families of more than one generation. The largest group is very often that of singles. This group is composed not only of young unmarried and those who are divorced or widowed, but individual members of families in which they are the only believer. Thus many people in the western churches suffer from loneliness and isolation. This presents both a challenge and an opportunity for the church to create a community of support for those who are the casualties of modern western society. There is, however, all too little evidence that the churches have so far responded creatively to this need.

The Churches' Emphasis

The churches, far from standing against the fragmentation of society, or being positively involved in the creation of community, have inadvertently aided the process of individuation by the evangelical emphasis upon the individual basis of salvation and the insistence that we are not Christians simply by being born into a Christian family, that each one has to make an individual confession of faith and an individual commitment to Christ. Evangelical teaching also includes a strong emphasis upon discipleship, personal maturity, personal righteousness and the accountability of each individual before God. Such teaching is soundly based upon the Gospel when taken in the context of western society's emphasis upon the individual and the general fragmentation of secular society, but it can lead to a very individualistic outworking of the faith that is contrary to New Testament teaching where the newest convert was immediately incorporated into the community of believers.

The western emphasis upon individual rights and individual achievement also produces individual pride

151

which not only militates against pride in the community but also produces spiritual pride and self-righteousness that makes it very difficult for individuals to submit to one another. It even militates against submission to the Lordship of Christ. Most western Christians do not even realise the extent to which their faith and practice are influenced by western individualism, which is one of the subtlest forms of spiritual pride.

In isolated instances, the church has recognised something of what has been happening and has been trying to recreate community. Most of the churches in the United Kingdom are modelled on the 'parish concept', which is a geographical model of community that is becoming increasingly difficult to maintain in a modern urban industrial nation. Gone are the days when each parish was a neighbourhood community of a *gemeinschaft* type – simple, closed and self-sufficient. Now many are of the *gesselschaft* type – complex, impersonal and not providing the same support for individuals as earlier forms of pre-industrial community.

Changing Community Concepts
This change in the structure of society requires a different policy from the church if it is going to provide a meaningful community. Too often, it has failed to make the change and not even realised why it has failed. The churches of the more non-conformist traditions although still to some extent copying the neighbourhood parish system have had more success with the 'gathered church', which is the basis of most churches in America. With this kind of concept, the church can uninhibitedly concentrate on the 'interest group' or the 'homogeneous unit principle' so that it can draw like-minded people together. This kind of community concentrates much more on members 'opting into' a community whether it is one of social-class, of interest, or of beliefs, rather than their being part of a natural community such as tribe, or neighbourhood.

Westerners have the freedom to choose whether or not they want to belong to a particular group, and also whom they want to exclude. They take pride in the Church being a community within the wider community of society-at-large, but often there are unspoken barriers limiting who may belong so that no one from the wider geographical community feels comfortable in the Church. The church members gain an increasing sense of isolation from secular society. As a consequence, many Christians feel no responsibility for what is happening in their own nation or in the world of international affairs.

This was highlighted for me recently when I was with a group of Christians in Britain, who were praying about the state of the nation and feeling moved to repent, not so much for the things which they personally had done, but more for the collective responsibility of the Church for the present state of the nation. Their particular concern was for the things which the Church had *not* done to guide the nation – its failure to speak out the Word of God or to stand against permissive legislation. One evangelical minister remonstrated that he could not repent in this way as he had done nothing wrong. He had lived an upright life and could bear no responsibility for the state of the nation of which he was a part – surely a prime example of western individualism!

Historical Perspectives

The simplest definition of a community is that of a group of people of both sexes and different ages covering several generations who recognise some form of common identity, kinship or belongingness that involves mutual rights and obligations. The most common form of community is geographical, but other valid forms of community may be communities of 'shared interest', such as professional associations, recreational groups or religious fellowships. Community is endemic to the church. It was an important part of New Testament Christianity as will be seen in the biblical witness section of this chapter.

Christian Rome

The impact of the Gospel upon the very different peoples of the Roman world was actually to create community out of diversity. The social structure of the Roman Empire provided an ideal background for the establishment of the church as a community of believers under the leadership of Christ. The basis of Roman social order was found in the 'Household System' which was a type of clan headed by the householder, who gathered around him close relatives, friends and a variety of retainers, servants and slaves all owing allegiance to the household and loyalty to its head. The whole Empire was composed of such households, some of which were extremely large and powerful. Each province was organised on a similar basis and was, in essence, a household unit recognising allegiance to Rome and to the Emperor himself as the overall head of the household that comprised the Empire.

The Church as a family of believers under the leadership of Christ related easily to the Roman household system with slaves and masters all in one community unit recognising common loyalty and belongingness in Christ. Thus, although the Church was proscribed for the first two centuries, its basic ethos was by no means alien to the Roman world. The Church was persecuted because of its insistence upon the headship of Christ: that Jesus, not Caesar, was Lord. With the conversion of Constantine, the policy of persecuting the Christians, pursued by his father, was reversed, but the social impact upon the Empire of this official change of religion was not so radical as may be imagined because the concept of community underlying the Church was so similar to that of the

Empire. It simply required the Emperor's acknowledgement of the Lordship of Jesus, for the secular Roman Empire to open the way for the establishment of the 'holy Roman Empire'.

While in theory this should have led to the evangelisation of all the peoples of the Empire, it also opened the way for the secularisation of the Church. It is for this reason that many church historians looking back to the conversion of Constantine in AD 316 regard it as a mixed blessing: either as a day of the greatest advancement for the Gospel, or of the greatest tragedy for the church. Certainly it was a turning point in church history. Discipleship changed from individual commitment to Christ, to belongingness to the Empire as part of that commitment. The concept of the Church changed from that of an exclusive community to that of an inclusive community; from a particularist ethic to a universalist ethic; from a community into which one opted to belong, to one into which one was automatically incorporated by birth.

Whether, in the fourth or fifth centuries AD, the Church succeeded in Christianising the Empire, or the Empire succeeded in secularising the church, is clearly a matter of debate, but it highlights the major problem of Christian evangelism throughout the centuries. Ever since Jesus gave the Great Commission to the church 'to make disciples of all nations', the objective of mission has been that of the evangelisation of whole nations. Every Christian longs to see his own nation come under the Lordship of Jesus, just as Paul longed to see the whole of Israel acknowledge Christ (Romans 11:26). But the moment whole nations acknowledge Christianity as the official religion, the State becomes involved, and political and economic interests begin to exert an influence upon the presentation of the Gospel. The forces of secularisation begin to take their toll as the interests of the State take precedence over the primary interests of the Gospel.

The Nature of the Kingdom

Maybe it is an essential part of the nature of the Church to be a minority community, standing out against the wider secular society in order to be the salt and light to the world, and thus fulfil the commandment of Jesus. This raises a question that is fundamental to mission strategies of world evangelisation as to the nature of the Kingdom. Jesus gave many illustrations of the different aspects of the Kingdom of God, some of which implied that the Kingdom may be realised in the 'here and now', and others that the Kingdom exists in a spiritual realm apart from this world. Jesus, in fact, said, 'My Kingdom is not of this world' (John 18:36), and yet he also taught his disciples to pray to the Father 'your Kingdom come, your will be done, *on earth* as it is in heaven' (Matt. 6:10).

These two apparently contradictory concepts of the Kingdom – which is both not of this world and yet begins here and now – highlight the Christian dilemma. We long to see the Kingdom of God established on earth but in the very moment of the apparent realisation of the Christian hope there comes the rude awakening that the essence of the Kingdom is spiritual, and is lost as soon as it becomes flesh.

Historically, the monastic movement was an attempt to answer this dilemma. It sought to establish Christian communities separated from the world but while monasticism made a great contribution to Christian thinking, to the preservation of truth and to theological learning, it also had a negative effect upon world evangelisation. It institutionalised the concept that the sacred could only remain pure in isolation from the secular. It established the idea that Christian community cannot exist in a secular environment.

The Reformation challenged this concept and attempted to re-define the church according to the New Testament pattern of the 'gathered church'. The church was seen as a 'community of believers' whose

primary commitment was to Christ, but who nevertheless recognised loyalty to the State, and the necessity
for the outworking of Christian faith in secular society
rather than in closed monastic communities.

The tension due to the conflicting interests of the
'secular' and the 'sacred' is a perennial problem for the
church. It no doubt accounts for such groups as the
Amish and Hutterite communities in the United
States who attempt to live an eighteenth-century
lifestyle as inter-dependent farming communities
under the Lordship of Jesus, but separated from the
trappings of the modern secular world.

Modern Communities
The desire to be separated from the corrupting
influences of secular society probably lies behind
much more of our current church life than is generally
recognised, and certainly more so than most Christians
would care to admit. This is to be seen in Britain, not
simply in distinct communities such as Bugbrook in
Northants, Post Green in Hampshire, Lee Abbey in
Devon or the Iona island community, but also in
many churches where there is a strong emphasis upon
the community life of the fellowship, and where the
members find all their needs are met; their friendships
and their social life are centred within the community
of the church. It may be that what we see developing
in Britain today is a new form of Christian separatism.

In its Victorian heyday, the Church was highly
involved in every aspect of the life of the nation not
only in the provision of education, hospitals and
caring services, but also in political affairs. But this
did not lead, as expected, to a 'nation under God' in
which every citizen was a committed Christian. In the
following generations what occurred was more akin to
the secularisation of the Gospel than the Christian-
isation of the nation. This raises the fundamental
question as to how far the Church can be successful in

getting the Gospel to permeate every aspect of the life of the nation without succumbing to the forces of secularisation or losing its own unique identity as a community of believers under the headship of Christ.

It may be that the answer lies in the basic difference between the western concept of community, and the biblical concept of community. The New Testament understanding of community is derived from the Hebrew concept of the 'corporate personality' of the nation under God, whom he called 'Israel, my Son'. In ancient Israel, the individual only had significance as part of the group – family, tribe or nation. Hence, when Aachan sinned the whole nation came under judgment. When the sin was traced to him there was no question of Aachan bearing individual responsibility and suffering punishment alone; his whole family were punished (Joshua 7:25). Such a concept is anathema to the western mind where each individual is deemed to be responsible for his own behaviour and there is no concept of shared responsibility.

The western understanding of community is that of a collection of individuals who are together for some purpose, possibly through shared interest, for the achievement of a particular goal or even through neighbourhood proximity, but who nevertheless each maintain their separate identity as individuals. Westerners, therefore, find it very difficult to appreciate the New Testament concept of the church as the Body of Christ – a community of believers; the people of God who were once not a community but who have been brought into a new and living relationship with God and with each other through the precious blood of the Lord Jesus.

Biblical Witness

Koinonia

The concept of the church presented in the New

Testament is that of a community of believers under the headship of Christ. The community of believers began at Pentecost with the shared experience of the upper room. The believers were conscious of the uniqueness of their mission as witnesses to the resurrection of Jesus, and as those who had been entrusted with a message to be carried to all nations. Acts 2:42 lists four key elements of community in the Jerusalem church. They were teaching, fellowship, the eucharist and prayer. The term *koinonia* or 'fellowship' expresses the heart of the new relationship between believers created by their shared allegiance to Christ. As they listened to the teaching of the apostles and as they worshipped and prayed together their community life deepened and became a visible expression of the life of the risen Christ.

As the number of believers grew rapidly, the sense of community deepened with the daily evidence of the presence of the risen Christ among them. 'Everyone was filled with awe and many wonders and miraculous signs were done by the apostles. All the believers were together and had everything in common' (Acts 2:43–44). The common belongingness that created the sense of community among the believers lay not only in their shared experience but in their common loyalty to Jesus. It was this that drove them to share their possessions. The persecution of the church by the authorities further served to strengthen the common bonds within the community.

The Body of Christ
Paul emphasises the quality of belongingness as a major characteristic of the church. He uses the illustration of a human body to describe the Church saying that just as the body has different parts performing different functions each of which are necessary for a healthy body and for the performance of all the functions of the human body, in the same

159

way each believer, although having a separate identity and different gifts, is an important part of the church and plays an essential function. He sees the Church as the body of Christ with each believer joined to the others with Christ as the head. He sees 'the whole body joined and held together by every supporting ligament and that it grows and builds itself up in love as each part does its work' (Eph. 4:16). Paul sees love as being the key to unity within the Church, and it is for this reason that he urges every member to be humble and gentle, to think more highly of each other and 'to bear with one another in love' (Eph. 4:2). The members should bear one another's burdens and 'be kind and compassionate to one another' (Eph. 4:32) in order to build up the body of Christ.

Paul emphasises the need for every member to share in the responsibility for building up the body of Christ, i.e. strengthening the community of believers. He sometimes refers to the Church as a building. 'For we are the temple of the living God. As God has said, "I will live with them and walk among them and I will be their God, and they will be my people"' (2 Cor. 6:16). The term Paul uses for 'building up' is the word *oikodome* which is derived from the noun *oikos* meaning a house. In the Roman world a house was not simply a building but a family, a household, a community of people recognising common loyalty to the head of household. This was Paul's concept of the Church. It was essentially a family in which relationships of love and mutual support among the members were essential.

Paul believed that the key to the relationships of belongingness among the members, lay in their common loyalty to Christ as their head. The members were to love one another in the same way as 'Christ loved the Church and gave himself up for her' (Eph. 5:25). Each believer was linked in a bond of love to Christ as a response to his love. 'We love because he first loved us'

(1 John 4:19). This was the essence of the covenant relationship between Christ and the Church. This covenant relationship, the church inherited from Israel.

The Covenant with God
The covenant which God first made with Abraham, and then in the time of Moses established with the whole nation of Israel, lay at the heart of the relationship between Israel and God. It was summarised in the words, 'I will be your God and you will be my people' (Lev. 26:12). Through this, Israel not only knew herself to have been chosen by God but also to have entered into a relationship with mutual rights and obligations. It was this special relationship with God that was the essential bond of unity among the twelve tribes of Israel. The covenant not only carried the privileges of a special relationship with God but also the obligations of obedience, loyalty and the fulfilment of a mission.

God had a purpose in calling Israel into a special relationship with himself. They were to be 'a light to the Gentiles' (Isaiah 49:6), through whom he would work out his purposes among all the nations. It was this mission, unfulfilled by the old Israel, that was inherited by the Church and, through Christ, the special covenant relationship was extended to the Church. Paul saw that it was God's intention to reveal himself to all the nations through the church. He saw that through Christ, God had broken down the barrier between Jew and Gentile, and that 'through the Gospel, the Gentiles are heirs together with Israel, members together of one body, and sharers together in the promise in Christ Jesus' (Eph. 3:6).

Inclusive Community
The Church, according to Paul's teaching, was a community of believers in which Christ had broken down all the human barriers of race, nationality and

161

kinship, and had even severed the differences in social rank and those between the sexes. He says, 'All of you who were baptised into Christ have been clothed with Christ. There is neither Jew nor Greek, slave nor free, male nor female, for you are all one in Christ Jesus' (Gal. 3:28). Paul saw this working out practically so that within the community of believers there had to be equality of status, all the members were to regard one another as brothers and sisters in Christ, hence his appeal to Philemon to receive back his runaway slave Onesimus 'no longer as a slave, but better than a slave, as a dear brother' (Philemon 1:16).

The Church brought together people of different nationality, race, and social rank, those who previously had no common identity, and formed them into a community. Peter acknowledges this in the words, 'Once you were not a people, but now you are the people of God' (1 Peter 2:10). This expresses the essential characteristic of the Church as a community of believers belonging to God, and brought into this special relationship through the Lord Jesus Christ.

Underlying Principles

One of the major principles coming out of this chapter on community consciousness is the need for the Church to concentrate much more on *belongingness*. Although western society has become increasingly individualistic, underneath the facade of self-sufficiency and independence there is an urgent need to belong. Society has become fragmented to such an extent that it can no longer provide the sense of fulfilment in relationships with others that everyone needs. The Church is in a unique position to help fill this need and to add the missing spiritual dimension to many people's lives. With its understanding of the body of Christ as a community of believers, it needs to give priority to the building up of such communities.

162

Another principle apparent in this section is that of the need to get the individual into a right perspective in line with the whole of God's creation. When self and personal needs come before Christ and the needs of others, whether in the church or outside, we are in danger. There needs to be a fresh emphasis upon the *negation of self*. Christians need to be encouraged to work for the *common good* rather than to think of everything in terms of personal advantage. The personal relationship of each individual with God is important, but that should not be the only concern of Christians. The personal relationship with God is for the purpose of serving him, and not solely for personal sanctification.

The principle of *caring* is one which needs to be given greater priority within the Church. The command of Christ to love one another, means not just those who love us – those who are like us or members of our own local church (although these personal relationships are very important), but also requires us to love those who do not love us, or who dislike us. The first step to loving others is to care for them. There is no substitute for caring; for the serving heart which has no thought of personal gain or of receiving in return. New Testament teaching requires believers to care for others because Christ first loved us even while we were yet sinners.

A further important principle is that of the *headship of Christ* in the church and in the life of every believer. Western Christians, with their emphasis on the freedom of the individual, do not find it easy to accept authority. Within the churches, authority is sometimes used in a way that usurps the headship of Christ. In some western churches there are wrong concepts of submission both to God and to each other. There is a need for the development of the servant quality of leadership in which both leaders and others are firmly under the headship of Christ.

Questions

1 What are the major causes of the fragmentation of community in the western nations?

2 How far is western individualism a product of the belief in the personal basis of salvation?

3 The 'parish church' is based upon a geographical community whereas the 'gathered church' is based upon a homogeneous community of interest. Does it follow that the former produces an inclusive type of community whereas the latter produces an exclusive community?

4 Does involvement in community activities pave the way for Christianising the nation or does it lead to the secularising of the Church?

5 Is the *koinonia* (Acts 2:44–45), which described the fellowship of common belongingness among believers in the earliest days of the Church, impracticable in today's world?

6 Is it easier for those who are used to natural forms of community to appreciate the New Testament teaching on the Church as a body of believers under the Headship of Christ with each individual having an ascribed place within the church community?

7 What were the characteristics of community in the New Testament church such as 'bearing one another's burdens' (Gal. 6:2) and 'Be devoted to one another in brotherly love. Honour one another above yourselves' (Romans 12:10)? Are these achievable in the church today? Do you see them in your own church?

8 The underlying principles linked with community consciousness discussed in this chapter are belongingness, negation of self, caring and the Headship of Christ. Can you discern any others?

Chapter Eight

What About the Poor?

*One man appears to be rich, yet has nothing;
another appears to be poor, yet has great wealth.*

Proverbs 13:7

The outstanding fact to emerge from any contemporary study of the worldwide church is that the growth, the spiritual power, the confidence and the blessings are all to be found among the non-western nations. Why should this be so, and what lessons are there for Christians in the western nations?

Growth in numbers is, of course, not necessarily a sign of God's blessing. If growth in numbers were always the test of the rightness of a movement, the tremendous growth of Communism, Secular Humanism and Islam during this century would be seen as moves of God. Jesus spoke about the weeds growing with the good corn until the time of harvest. What we are seeing today is the rapid growth of the Kingdom in many nations, but also the continuing increase of forces diametrically opposed to the Kingdom; the two are growing together.

In Matthew 24, verses 5 to 14, Jesus foresaw the time coming when the Gospel would be preached to people in all the nations. He also spoke of this as a time when there would be strong forces of evil in the world, including false Christs and false prophets. He said that it would not only be a time of violence among the nations with wars and rumours of wars and a time of natural disasters with famines and earthquakes, but it would also be a time of the persecution of believers when many would be put to death and others would 'turn away from the faith' and 'betray and hate each other'. In Jesus' teaching, the time of worldwide evangelism coincides with a period of international tension and turmoil which would also be linked to persecution of the faithful and apostasy in the Church. The great falling away from the faith that has taken place in Europe during the twentieth century can hardly be described other than as a time of apostasy.

Jesus also linked the increase of wickedness with a lack of love among believers. He said that 'because of the increase of wickedness, the love of most will grow cold'. One of the things that John warned the Church at Ephesus about was a lack of love – 'You have forsaken your first love. Remember the height from which you have fallen! Repent and do the things you did at first' (Rev. 2:4–5). The first love of the believer has to be the love of God and love for the Lord Jesus. The love of the believer is a response to the love of the Father. 'We love him because he first loved us' (1 John 4:19). If the Church ever loses sight of what God in Christ has done for us, then love will grow cold. Maybe this is what has happened to the churches in Europe, whereas, in contrast, churches in Third World countries are still in their first love and are vibrant with faith.

Faithlessness

It is this faith in God that is the key to an understanding of what is happening in many nations where the Gospel is spreading rapidly. Faith is the confident expectation that God will fulfil his promises, and that he is faithful under all circumstances. Such faith gives confidence to believers to know that even in times of persecution God is able to protect his people or to give them the courage to stand firm in the face of the violence of men, and to make a powerful witness to the love of God. He is able to turn even the apparent disaster of human suffering into a victory for the Kingdom, in the same way as he turned the death of Christ into the new life of resurrection.

Faith linked with expectation produces the most amazing results. The churches that are experiencing the most rapid and spectacular growth are led by men and women who have the absolute conviction that they are doing what God has told them to do and, therefore, he will bless their work. They expect to see multitudes respond to the Gospel, and lives changed. They expect the sick to be healed, the blind to see and the lame to walk, for these were the signs of the Kingdom that Jesus referred to in his message to John the Baptist. They do not look for healings simply out of a desire to see signs and wonders, but they expect such things to happen as a natural consequence of the Gospel being preached in the power of the Spirit, and the presence of the Lord coming down upon the people. When God is present the needs of his people are met. His blessings are poured out and the people rejoice, not so much in the miracles, but in the love and mercy of God and the joy that his presence among them brings.

It is this lack of the expectation of the activity of God that is the greatest barrier to growth in the Church in Britain, and in many other western nations. Christians really do not expect God to do anything spectacular in their individual lives, in the church, or in the nation. The 'God is Dead' movement among liberal theologians of the 1960s, although thoroughly discredited today, nevertheless left its mark upon the faith of the whole western church. It is a fact that the European churches, in particular, not only experienced a lack of growth but acutally saw the numbers attending church decline by more than a million a year through the 1960s and 1970s.

Inevitably, such decline creates a loss of confidence

167

that has a paralysing effect upon spiritual activity, and in the subtlest way creates a lack of trust in God. Leaders are afraid to commit themselves to large-scale planning that requires stepping out in faith. The result is that all thinking and planning is on a small scale and spiritual activity becomes dogged by the 'failure syndrome'. The timidity of leaders is communicated right through the body. Planning for the future is dominated by defensive thinking rather than the expectation of growth. Even the preaching of the Word focuses on the faithfulness of the remnant rather than on a message of hope such as that brought by Isaiah, 'Enlarge the place of your tent, stretch your tent curtains wide, do not hold back; lengthen your cords, strengthen your stakes. For you will spread out to the right and to the left' (Isaiah 54:2-3).

Lack of expectation is rooted in a lack of trust in God which stems from a poverty of faith. If there is a lack of faith in God, so, too, there is a lack of trust in God. It is faith that gives hope for the future and produces a trust in God that causes us to step out in faith – as Abraham went out not knowing where he was going but with absolute trust in God, whom he knew to be faithful. The believer who has experienced the love of God will be obedient even if he doesn't fully understand the implications of what he is hearing from God. If God says, 'Go', he will go in the confidence that he will not be alone, that God will go with him and that God also has the power to fulfil his promises and to accomplish his purpose. Faith and confidence in God are closely linked with personal experience, and it is this personal experience of the love of God and the power of God that has been mainly lacking in western churches during the lean years of the mid-twentieth century.

It is in this same period that faith, expectation and confidence have grown in the newer churches of the Third World. These churches have not been troubled to the same extent by intellectualism and the onslaught of secular humanism, as has been experienced in the West where even those churches that have remained faithful to the trustworthiness of Scripture have had their faith dulled by the battle. Fundamentalism, which is a phenomenon peculiar to the twentieth century, is essentially defensive in attitude, and a product of the 'seige mentality'. This does not, of course, mean that defenders cannot be aggressive! Those whose energies are fully absorbed in defending the status quo are unlikely to produce creative policies that will lead to great adventures of faith, confident expectation and joyful anticipation of all that God will do.

Intellectualism has had its effect upon the whole church; no sector can claim to have been untouched. The Pentecostal movement of the 1920s was essentially creative in emphasising the presence and power of the Holy Spirit in the church where it had, for a long time, been neglected. As Pentecostalism moved into its third generation and began to emerge from its separatist policy, the desire to influence the wider body of the church and the desire for acceptance by other Christians produced a radical change in the policy of Pentecostal churches, particularly in their training programmes for pastors and leaders, which took on a greater academic emphasis. This was not simply due to the influence of the world, but to the desire to take their place alongside other churches as acceptable denominations with appropriate organisation and accreditation of ministers. This inevitably led to some dulling of the faith and spiritual creativity. Acceptance by the wider church is necessary for any movement to be able to share its spiritual insights, but there is a cost to acceptability. Pentecostals in Britain and America (although not so much on mainland Europe) have paid the price of acceptability but there can be no doubt that their loss has been gain to the wider church in the impetus given to the Charismatic movement, which has brought new life to the traditional denominations and older churches.

The Pentecostals went through their times of persecution, not from the world, but from the church. The form of persecution they experienced was not physical violence, but abuse, ridicule and rejection, all of which had the effect of increasing their 'separateness' and causing them to look to God as their only source of help and strength. Persecution has this effect upon believers, who are conscious of having been called by God to take a stand for truth and, therefore, their trust is in the Lord and not in man. God is their defender. The persecuted believers stake their faith and sometimes even their lives upon the belief that 'God is our refuge and strength, an ever-present help in trouble. Therefore we will not fear' (Psalm 46:1-2). The actual experience of the presence of God, his protection and his enabling power in times of trouble, strengthens the faith of believers and actually enables God to accomplish mighty things through them, which, in turn, leads to a further strengthening of their confidence in God. This becomes a 'growth spiral' which is the antithesis of the 'failure syndrome' to which previous reference has been made.

This is what has happened in China, and it is happening today in many other nations where there is active opposition to the Gospel. By contrast, nations in the western world, who boast of their tolerance, often react with apathy towards Christians in the traditional sectors of the church, and with scorn and incredulity towards those whose faith is more actively and fervently expressed. The outstanding mark of Christians in the persecuted church is that of commitment to Christ and of obedience to him under all circumstances, even to the cost of their personal freedom or to the ultimate sacrifice of life itself. For Christians in the West, whose commitment and self-sacrifice is not met with violent opposition, this can sometimes result in the gradual softening of commitment and wearing down of perseverance. Faith and practice become routine and even obedience becomes dull and dutiful. Persecution acts as a honing stone sharpening the sword of the Spirit in the hand of the believer, whereas social tolerance and apathy have a dulling effect.

Christians in the persecuted churches constantly see the power of God among them. They have the same confidence as Paul had when he was standing up against great opposition to the Gospel, and had 'learned to be content whatever the circumstances'. He declared, 'I can do everything through him who gives me strength' (Phil. 4:11-13). By contrast, Christians in many churches in the West rarely see anything remotely resembling the power of God at work. Even if they do, they are often like those of whom Ezekiel said, 'They have eyes to see but do not see and ears to hear but do not hear' (Ezekiel 12:2).

Powerlessness

Western Christians do not share the experience of Paul because they do not have his faith to believe that God can move mountains and totally transform even the most hopeless of situations. Paul actually boasted in his weakness, for he knew that in the acknowledgement of his own powerlessness and the almighty power of God, God could enter and transform the situation. Many western Christians accept their spiritual powerlessness as a sign of the powerlessness of God in the contemporary world, and therefore are not open to the confident expectation of a demonstration of his power, such as Paul experienced when he preached the Gospel at Corinth (1 Cor. 2:4).

Western theologians have reduced God to an intellectual concept. He is the 'essence of all being' who exists in the shadowy world of philosophical concepts. Thus he is far removed from the personal God of

Scripture, who was Abraham's friend, who spoke face to face with Moses, in whose presence the prophets learned to stand, and who perfectly revealed himself in Jesus the incarnate Son of God. God does not normally work in the context of faithlessness and unbelief, especially among those who have had the Word of Life, who have known the truth but have denied it and turned their backs upon God. They are regarded by God as a rebellious people, which was the charge made by Ezekiel after his statement that they neither used their eyes nor their ears. This was also the reason why Jesus refused to give a miraculous sign to unbelievers. They simply would not believe with their hearts even if they saw with their eyes. Jesus saw no reason to cast spiritual pearls before swine.

For the western churches to experience the power of God flowing through the institutional life of the church and out into the nation, there must first be an openness to change as well as the recognition of powerlessness. It is not sufficient simply to acknowledge our powerlessness, which may be accepted as the norm or as something over which we have no control, there has also to be the recognition that God does not wish his church to remain in a state of powerlessness and there has to be the openness to change that allows God to act.

Christians in the West need to realise that they do not have to struggle on bravely trying to maintain the witness of the church in an increasingly secular and apathetic society. Christians are not on their own in a hostile world. God has provided the power for the battle against all the forces of darkness, but that power has to be received. It can only be transmitted into the Church through an acknowledgement of the headship of Christ; that it is *his* church, not ours. The Church is not simply a human institution depending upon the organising ability of man for its maintenance and the successful carrying out of its mission. When Christ is acknowledged as the head of the Church, the authority lies with him and he is then able to direct its affairs.

The headship of Christ also ensures that human beings do not take the credit for divine acts of power. Paul instructed the Corinthians that whatever they did they should 'do it all for the glory of God' (1 Cor. 10:31), and Jesus was careful to acknowledge the Father in everything that he did. 'The Son can do nothing by himself', he said. 'He can do only what he sees his Father doing' (John 5:19). Jesus gave all the glory to the Father and this was the spiritual principle he laid down for the lives of his disciples. He said, 'This is to my Father's glory, that you bear much fruit, showing yourselves to be my disciples' (John 15:8). Because Jesus gives all the glory to the Father, when he is acknowledged as head of the Church, all the evidence of his power working through believers brings glory to God. It is not the servant who is exalted but the Master, and this is the safety-net for true disciples that prevents them falling into the pit of pride and self-esteem.

In fact, self-negation is the mark of the true disciple, who has no desire to promote his own name or elevate his own reputation, but rather is jealous for the reputation of Christ and is keen to give all the glory to God. In many ways this is easier for Christians in Third World churches who do not have a vast store of material resources or monetary wealth. They have to rely on the provision of God and upon his power to overcome their lack of resources. They readily acknowledge their need and when God provides in abundance, their joy overflows in praise and wonder at the mercy, love and bounty of the Father.

Western Christians, by contrast, are used to having an immense store of physical resources and human expertise at their disposal, which leads many churches to think in terms of cheque-book Christianity – an attitude of mind that believes or thinks that everything can be purchased, that all things are possible to him who has; and unto him who has, more shall be added! The accumulation of wealth in investments, in the ownership of property, the acquisition of land and priceless treasures and works of art is one of the major obscenities of the western church. How incongruous is the ownership of such wealth when the Lord Jesus, the head of the church, said, 'Foxes have holes and birds of the air have nests, but the Son of Man has no place to lay his head' (Matt. 8:20). It is not easy for leaders of the western churches, who have the responsibility for the administration of institutions owning such vast resources of wealth and power, to maintain a simplicity of faith, lifestyle, commitment to Christ and trust in God.

The institutional church, with its vast investment in the secular world, tends to think and to act in the same way as secular or worldly leaders. When faced with a problem, the first reaction of institutions is to find out what resources are available. Secondly, when it is apparent that there are insufficient resources available to deal with the problem, the institutional reaction is to set up a committee of enquiry. Western churches usually behave in the same way, and only rarely is the power of God included among the resources available, and only rarely is God consulted through the Holy Spirit for divine guidance to bring light to the situation.

Humility and simplicity of lifestyle are rarely a problem for Christians in the Third World, although where leaders get caught up in false teaching, such as the 'Prosperity Gospel', they may be tempted to follow western styles of affluence and resort to worldly behaviour, such as the flaunting of riches. True humility is unconcerned for self, shuns self-aggrandisement and deliberately points others away from self and towards Christ. Western Christians have a constant struggle to maintain the dominance of spiritual values over worldly and secular values. They are surrounded by a society whose values are at variance with those of the Gospel, that despises humility as weakness, and imposes values of competition at every level of human relationships.

Individualism

The competitiveness of western society is rooted in individualism. The drive to achieve and to succeed in life is instilled into children in the western nations from their earliest years. From their first encounter with nursery school, they are praised for achievement, and are taught to compete, even through the games they play. The acquisition of property on an individual basis is taught even to young children, through the giving of birthday presents and gifts, sometimes as a reward for good behaviour or achievement. Many children, even in wealthy families, are rewarded by money being given in return for doing simple jobs or acts of community service. In this way, children are taught the value of individual wages and that everything has to be earned. The net result is the emphasis upon the individual basis of society, which leads to institutionalised forms of self-centredness. It would not be true to say that Third World countries are free from the same corrupting forces of self-centredness that are characteristic of western society. In fact many forms of corruption, presently being practiced in Third World countries and despised in the West, owe their origins to western colonialism and commercialism.

Belongingness

The antithesis of western individualism lies in the establishment of a caring community where everyone gives greater honour to others and seeks the good of the whole community rather than the interests of self. These are the values of the Gospel that were embraced by the New Testament church, and were the cause of great joy in the days following Pentecost when the members of the Jerusalem church, according to Luke, 'devoted themselves to the apostles' teaching and to the fellowship, to the breaking of bread and to prayer . . . All the believers were together and had everything in common . . . They broke bread in their homes and ate together with glad and sincere hearts, praising God and enjoying the favour of all the people' (Acts 2:42–47).

Christians in Third World countries usually have a greater sense of community than Christians in the more individualised West. In those places where they are carrying over into the church their concept of community, plus a foundation of the values of the Kingdom as taught in the Gospel, strong fellowships of believers after the pattern of the New Testament church are resulting. Such communities not only show love and care in the relationships between the members, but also give a practical demonstration of unity to the world. The old tribal enmities between believers from different people groups are broken down through a common loyalty to Christ, and the consequent 'belongingness' not only to him as Lord of the church, but to each other as brothers and sisters in Christ.

This was the kind of community Paul described at Colossae. 'Here there is no Greek or Jew, circumcised or uncircumcised, barbarian or Scythian, slave or free, but Christ is all, and is in all' (Col 3:11). The kind of behaviour Paul expected within the community of Christ's people was 'compassion, kindness, humility, gentleness and patience'. He exhorted the Colossians to 'bear with each other and forgive whatever grievances you may have against one another' (v12–13). Many Christians in Third World countries are actually seeing this happen as new believers from different tribal backgrounds are coming into fellowship.

Western Christians, by contrast, are seeing the fragmentation of even such community as does exist in urban industrial societies. The forces of disintegration through continuing urban expansion, the high rate of marriage breakdown, and the steady erosion of family life, are accelerating rather than diminishing. The western churches have yet to discover the way of combating these disintegrating forces, and creatively promoting community renewal programmes. These will not only establish identity and belongingness among urban people used to individualism and loneliness, but will also establish spiritual values that promote the health and well-being both of individuals and community. Such communities will also help to re-establish the importance and centrality of family life. It is only the re-establishment of family life at the heart of the life of the nation that can overcome such injustices as the neglect of children and child abuse.

Justice and Injustice

These injustices are seen on an international scale in the malnutrition and disease that claims the lives of millions of infants and children in some of the poorest nations of the world every year. The initiative for overcoming the obscenity of injustice on such a vast scale has to come from western Christians, whose nations hold a monopoly of the world's wealth and power. It is these nations who have medical resources and expertise to give effective aid for the relief of suffering, and who also have the ability to help Third World nations to develop their natural resources and to become self-supporting. Justice demands that the rich do more than merely give aid as an act of charity to the casualties of an unjust system from which they continue to profit. 'Give a man a fish and you feed him for a day. Teach a man to fish and you feed him for life.' Although this is the ethos followed by many development agencies working in the Third World today, the truth underlying this old Chinese proverb needs to be learned by those who hold real political and economic power in the rich western nations if justice is to be established in the world.

In the fight to establish justice not only in their own communities but also worldwide, Christians have an important role to play as salt and light. They need to stand firmly against corruption and the evil forces of injustice, and thus act as salt in society. At the same time, they need to act as light through proclaiming the word of God and witnessing fearlessly to the standards of righteousness as given in the New Testament. The need is not simply to proclaim the truth in words, but also to establish communities in which justice can be seen to exist, and in which the relationships of love, unselfish service and care for one another characterise all the members. Such models of community represent the most powerful way of proclaiming the truth to unbelievers where secular society is full of fear and violence. They may also act as microcosms of truth that will spread through the nations, meeting the hunger of humanity for peace and harmony.

Need for a Whole Gospel

If justice is to be established in the world, it is essential for Christians both to believe and to proclaim the whole Gospel of Christ. Partiality is a common error of humanity. We seize upon one small element of truth and imagine we have the whole truth. We seize upon one part of the model and imagine we have grasped the whole. This is part of the arrogance of our humanity through which we convince ourselves that we are greater and more mature than we are. It is all part of the common human failing of elevating self. The Gospel deals with this not by putting us down but by elevating Christ; not by crushing our humanity but by transforming it through the renewing power of the Holy Spirit; not by saying that men and women are of no worth, but by saying that they are of supreme worth to God even to the extent of his giving his own Son for our salvation. It is only a whole Gospel that can set mankind free from the bondage of self, and liberate humanity from the effects of human selfishness and greed, and from the effects of violence and corruption that lead to the destruction of nations.

When the whole Gospel is proclaimed in word and in deed with the power and authority of the Holy Spirit as promised by Jesus, the power of God is released. This is what the New Testament means by signs and wonders following the preaching of the Word. This is currently the experience of Christian leaders and simple believers in many Third World countries, and it needs to be the shared experience of Christians throughout the world. The vision of the worldwide church fulfilling the Great Commission of its master will bring together East and West, North and South in a community of believers, communicating the Word of Life to the nations, demonstrating the power of God at work among his people, and bringing new hope to mankind.

Learning

Rich and poor each have something to contribute to the other for this vision to become a reality. It would, however, be simplistic to give the impression that what is being experienced in one part of the world is easily transferrable to another. There is no one blueprint. Methods working in one area rarely work in another. The differences in culture, tradition, background and circumstances often make this impossible. The underlying principles of truth can, however, be learned, as has already been noted in earlier chapters of this book and as we have been attempting to summarise in this chapter.

Clearly, Christians in Third World nations have

much to offer to the West through their vibrant faith and the new life and spiritual power they are experiencing as the blessings of God are poured out upon them. Paul's teaching was that the newest believers had something of value to be shared with mature believers. He told the Galatians, 'Anyone who receives instruction in the word, must share all good things with his instructor' (Gal. 6:6). In Paul's view, the teacher has as much to *receive* from the pupil as to give to him. No doubt he was referring to the latter's fresh spiritual experience, vitality and joy in the Lord.

Christians in the West not only have something to learn but also have much to contribute to their brothers and sisters in the materially poorer nations. Despite the barriers to growth and spiritual power, which have developed in the western nations particularly in the twentieth century, the churches in the West still have a rich spiritual heritage to give to the world.

The blocks to spiritual power and growth may be summarised as pride in freedom and tolerance as noted in the chapter on *Persecution*; over-confidence in self and material resources noted in the chapter on *Shaking and Revival*; the identification of Christianity with citizenship in the West and consequent apathy, noted in the chapter on *Growth in Numbers*; the over-emphasis on intellectualism and head-knowledge noted in the chapter on *Spiritual Power*; spiritual tunnel-vision and parochialism noted in the chapter on *Prophetic Witness*; and individualism noted in the chapter on *Community Consciousness*.

Each of these points are not essentially evil in themselves; they contain elements of truth, but when taken to excess or in isolation from the whole truth of the Gospel, they become error. For example, the western emphasis upon the individual and individual responsibility could be said to reflect the teaching of the Gospel on the value of each individual in the sight of God, and the fact that salvation is an individual experience; we come into new birth as individuals in the same way as we experience natural birth. Individualism becomes sin when it is carried to excess, and self becomes the centre of our world and we become consumed with pride and selfish ambition.

The western churches have centuries of tradition upon which to draw as part of their rich spiritual heritage. This should be seen as a gift from God to be shared with the whole Church. Tradition is a stabilising factor from which we learn from the experience of the past, both failures and successes, truth and error. Tradition also provides the present with an essential link to the past that gives continuity with the past and confidence for the future. It places us within God's time framework.

The West also has a wealth of biblical scholarship, devotion and piety, as well as vast material resources, to share with Christians in the Third World. Many Christians in the West have learned faithfulness under the most testing conditions of decline and apathy, and this has produced fortitude and perseverance as a valuable spiritual asset to be shared. Western Christians need to look at their whole Christian experience to see what can be offered as of value to others: what can cross the cultural barriers and be helpful, rejecting those which could bring problems in the future.

The point being emphasised is that both rich and poor have something valuable to share. Neither should feel useless or unwanted. Within the Body of Christ there are no inferior and superior Christians, there are no high-status and low-status believers. All are one in Christ, with different gifts to contribute to the world-wide growth of the Christian community.

Facing the Facts
This does not, however, mean that Christians in the West should feel complacent. There needs to be a

frank recognition of the fact that it is believers in the poorest nations who are experiencing the blessings of God. This is a living illustration of the teaching of Jesus that the Gospel turns upside-down the values of the world. It underlines the fact that in the Kingdom of God, the rich are the poor and the poor are the rich. God is concerned for all – that all should become rich in spiritual things.

Hope for the Future

Many Christians in the West are longing to see revival and are constant in their intercession for the renewing power of God to come upon the Church, and for a fresh outpouring of the Spirit of God upon their nations. Their cry to God is, 'Oh Lord, what about the poor? When will you revive the poor?' The response of the Spirit to the heartcry of believers in the West is, 'When you acknowledge that you are the poor, when you are willing to *receive* as well as to give, when you believe with the faith of a little child – then will I revive you.'